Westward Trails

Author: Cindy Barden
Editor: Mary Dieterich
Contributor: Karl Mechem
Proofreaders: April Hawkins and Maurita McCarthy

ISBN 978-1-62223-904-7

Printing No. CD-405090

Mark Twain Media, Inc., Publishers
Distributed by Carson Dellosa Education

Visit us at www.marktwainpublishing.com

Table of Contents

Introduction to the Teacher

Welcome to *Westward Trails,* one of the books in the Mark Twain Media, Inc., American History series for students in grades 5–8+.

The activity books in this series are designed as stand-alone material for classrooms and home-schoolers or as supplemental material to enhance your history curriculum. Students can be encouraged to use the books as independent study units to improve their understanding of historical events and people. Teachers or parents should make the necessary copies of the reproducible activities if multiple students will be using the materials.

This book provides challenging activities that enable students to explore history, geography, and social studies topics. The activities provide research opportunities and promote critical reading, thinking, and writing skills. As students follow the journeys of settlers and learn about the people and events involved in the settlement of the West, they will draw conclusions; write opinions; compare and contrast historical events, people, and places; analyze cause and effect; and improve mapping skills. Students will also have the opportunity to apply what they learn to their own lives through reflection and creative writing.

Students can further increase their knowledge and understanding of historical events by using reference sources at the library and on the Internet. Students may need assistance to learn how to use search engines and discover appropriate websites.

Titles of books for additional reading appropriate to the subject matter at this grade level are included at the back of the book.

Although many of the questions are open-ended, answer keys are included at the back of the book for questions with specific answers.

Time Line of the Westward Trails

1804–1806 The Lewis and Clark Expedition explored the country for a water route to the Pacific Ocean.

1806 Zebulon Pike explored most of the Santa Fe Trail route.

1812 Louisiana became a state.

1816 Indiana became a state.

1817 Mississippi became a state.

1818 Illinois became a state.

1821 Missouri became a state.

1826 Jedediah Smith led the first party of Americans overland to California.

Major George Sibley completed the first survey of the Santa Fe Trail.

1827 Dr. John McLoughlin built the first lumber mill in the Pacific Northwest at Fort Vancouver.

1828 Andrew Jackson was elected president.

1831–1838 The forced removal of Native Americans from the East to Oklahoma occurred. This was later called the "Trail of Tears."

1836 Arkansas became a state.

1837 Michigan became a state.

1840 William Henry Harrison was elected president.

1841 John Bidwell organized the Western Emigration Society.

William Henry Harrison died; John Tyler became president.

1842 Don Francisco Lopez discovered gold in the roots of an onion at Placerita Canyon in the San Fernando Valley.

1843 Jim Bridger and Louis Vasquez established Fort Bridger.

Free land in Oregon sparks "Oregon Fever."

The "Great Migration": 1,000 pioneers left Independence, Missouri, on a 2,000-mile journey to the Willamette Valley.

1844 Joseph Smith, the founder of the Church of Jesus Christ of Latter-day Saints (often called the Mormon Church), was killed in Carthage, Illinois.

Brigham Young became the new leader of the Church of Jesus Christ of Latter-day Saints.

James K. Polk was elected president.

The first long distance telegram was sent.

1845 Florida became a state.

Texas became a state.

1846 Oregon Territory became a part of the United States.

The Latter-day Saints were forced to leave Nauvoo, Illinois.

The Donner Party met disaster.

Iowa became a state.

1846–1848 The Mexican War was fought.

Time Line of the Westward Trails

1847 Members of the Church of Jesus Christ of Latter-day Saints established Salt Lake City.

1848 James Marshall discovered gold while building a lumber mill for John Sutter.

The United States gained Arizona, California, Nevada, New Mexico, Utah, and western Colorado from Mexico after the Mexican War.

Zachary Taylor was elected president.

Wisconsin became a state.

1849 The first ship carrying prospectors arrived in California.

Wagon trains with approximately 20,000 people headed for the Gold Rush.

1850 President Taylor died; Millard Fillmore became president.

California became a state.

The Land Donation Act was passed.

1852 Franklin Pierce was elected president.

1853 The Gadsden Purchase was acquired from Mexico for $10 million.

1856 The first American camel expedition set out from Texas.

James Buchanan was elected president.

1858 Minnesota became a state.

1859 Oregon became a state.

1860 The first Pony Express rider left St. Joseph, Missouri.

Abraham Lincoln was elected president.

1861 The Civil War began.

Transcontinental telegraph service began. Pony Express service ended.

Kansas became a state.

1862 The Homestead Act was passed.

1863 West Virginia became a state.

1864 President Lincoln was reelected.

Nevada became a state.

1865 President Lincoln was assassinated; Andrew Johnson became president. The Civil War ended.

1867 Alaska was purchased from Russia for $7.2 million in gold.

Nebraska became a state.

1868 Ulysses S. Grant was elected president.

1869 The Transcontinental Railroad was completed.

Major John Powell began exploration of the Colorado River.

1872 Yellowstone became the first national park.

President Grant was reelected.

A railroad was completed to the Colorado border, ending the use of the Santa Fe Trail by most travelers.

Name: ________________________ Date: ________________

The Trails Led West

Pioneers who traveled west followed Native American trade routes and hunting trails that had been used for centuries. However, no Native American trail led all the way from Missouri to Santa Fe, California, or Oregon. By the late 1830s, mountain men and explorers like Kit Carson, Jim Bridger, Zebulon Pike, and Tom Fitzpatrick had explored most of the routes.

Kit Carson

Jim Bridger

Zebulon Pike

Select one option:

A. Write a report that includes maps and illustrations of routes explored by mountain men.

B. Use reference sources. Write an essay on the influence of mountain men on the Oregon or Santa Fe Trail.

C. Write a tall tale about a mountain man or woman. Include illustrations.

Beginning in 1840, people started moving west in large numbers. Members of the "Emigrant Societies" helped establish passable overland trails to the West and wrote guidebooks for travelers.

The first wagon train, known as the Bidwell-Bartleson party, included 69 people who left Missouri in the spring of 1841. The group went as far as Soda Springs, Idaho; there they split up. Some went to Oregon and others to California.

Most trails to the West began at Independence or St. Joseph, Missouri, or Council Bluffs, Iowa. There were three major overland trails used by most people. Depending on their final destination, most groups took either the Oregon Trail, the California Trail, or the Santa Fe Trail. Each trail had several variations.

Those traveling in wagon trains had to take routes that were not the most direct because of several natural obstacles: the canyons of Colorado, the Sierra Nevada Mountains, and the deserts around the Great Salt Lake.

Travelers faced many obstacles along the trails, including hills and mountains, streams and rivers, deserts, extremes of temperature, and attacks by some groups of Native Americans who resented the intrusion into their lands.

Name: ______________________________ Date: ____________________

Manifest Destiny

Once it became an independent nation, the United States experienced a rapid increase in population due to immigration and a high birthrate. Since agriculture was the basis for the economic structure of the country, large families to work the farms were an asset. The U.S. population grew from more than five million in 1800, to more than 23 million by mid-century.

This population explosion increased the need to expand into new territory. As parts of the Louisiana Territory became settled, ordinary Americans began walking, riding, and driving wagons over the immense mountains to reach the fertile farmlands of Oregon and California. Some historians estimate that nearly 4,000,000 Americans moved to western territories between 1820 and 1850.

In 1845, a New York editor wrote: "It is America's **'Manifest Destiny'** to overspread and to possess the whole of the continent which Providence has given us for the development of the great experiment of Liberty and federated self-government entrusted to us."

Americans believed that Manifest Destiny was both a right and an obligation. However, the rights of Native Americans who lived in the same areas were ignored. Those who resisted were either forcibly removed or killed.

Frontier land was usually inexpensive, and sometimes even free, promising a better life for those who didn't own land. Some people moved west simply because they desired adventure. The discovery of gold in California in 1848 and the completion of the Transcontinental Railroad in 1869 were other factors that attracted people to the West.

1. Use a dictionary to define the following words.

   Manifest ____

   ____

   Destiny ____

   ____

2. Explain in your own words what you think the New York editor meant.

   ____

   ____

   ____

   ____

   ____

   ____

Name: ______________________ Date: ______________

Moving West

When people decided to join a wagon train and follow the Santa Fe or Oregon Trail, they had to leave many of their possessions behind. They knew they might never see their friends and relatives again. So why did people travel 2,000 miles or more to get to Oregon? Were they traveling *to* something or *away from* something?

Some went to take advantage of the free farmland available. Some hoped for a better life and a new start. Some searched for adventures and new experiences. Others wanted to escape problems at home.

When the pioneers traveled west, they knew there was little chance they would ever return. When people today move a long distance, they can return for visits. Most places in the United States can be reached by airplane in only a few hours. We also have other ways to keep in touch that weren't available to the pioneers.

1. List five reasons why people today might move to a new state. Be specific.

____

____

____

____

____

2. Who or what would you miss most if your family moved to another state? Why?

____

____

____

3. List ways people today keep in touch with friends and relatives who live far away.

____

____

____

4. If your family planned to move to another state, in which state would you most like to live? Why?

____

____

____

Name: ______________________ Date: ______________

From Missouri to Santa Fe

The Old Santa Fe Trail, **painting by Frederic Remington**

Santa Fe was one of the first European settlements in what later became the United States.

The Santa Fe Trail was used regularly by traders beginning in 1821. From Independence, Missouri, to Santa Fe, New Mexico, the trail was about 780 miles long.

Settlers who followed the trail traveled west to the Arkansas River and then continued southwest along the river. The Santa Fe Trail offered two options; travelers could continue along the river to Bent's Fort in Colorado and then head south through Raton Pass to Santa Fe. The other route led across the Cimarron Desert.

The Cimarron Cutoff was shorter and easier for people traveling in covered wagons, but the risk of attack by Native Americans was higher, and water was scarce.

Merchant-traders traveled back and forth along the Santa Fe Trail with wagons or mule trains. Santa Fe was a major trading area where goods from Missouri could be exchanged for furs and other items.

Some people went to Santa Fe to make their homes and open businesses. Those who wanted to continue on could take either the Old Spanish Trail, which led to Los Angeles, or the El Camino Real, a trail south to Mexico City.

In 1880, the railroad reached Santa Fe, and use of the Santa Fe Trail declined.

Use reference sources to complete this page.

1. People from what country founded Santa Fe in 1610? ______________
2. In 1821, Santa Fe became part of a different country. What country claimed Santa Fe after 1821? ______________
3. After 1848, Santa Fe became part of the United States. Why? ______________

   ____
4. What is a mule train? ______________

   ____
5. Why do you think few people traveled along the Santa Fe Trail after the railroad connected Santa Fe with the eastern part of the United States?

   ____

   ____

Name: ______________________________ Date: ____________________

Along the Santa Fe Trail

Use the map of the Santa Fe Trail on the next page to complete this activity.

1. Trace the Santa Fe Trail in red on the map.
2. The Santa Fe Trail cut across four different states. Name them.

   ____

   ____

Those bound for Santa Fe had two choices. The Mountain Route followed the Arkansas River into Colorado before turning south. The Cimarron Cutoff crossed a waterless desert, but it saved about ten days' travel.

3. Trace the Cimarron Cutoff in red.
4. Does the Cimarron Cutoff appear to be a longer or shorter way to go to Santa Fe?

   ____

5. By taking the Cimarron Cutoff, what state did travelers enter that they didn't enter if they took the Mountain Route?

   ____

6. What rivers did the Cimarron Cutoff cross?

   ____

Name the state along the Santa Fe Trail where each place is located.

7. Bent's Old Fort ____________________
8. Bent's New Fort ____________________
9. San Miguel ____________________
10. Canadian Crossing ____________________
11. Caches ____________________
12. Fort Zarah ____________________
13. Independence ____________________
14. Trinidad ____________________
15. Diamond Spring ____________________

Bent's Old Fort National Historic Site

Name: ________________________________ Date: ________________________

Along the Santa Fe Trail Map

Use this map of the Santa Fe Trail to complete the activities on pages 8 and 16.

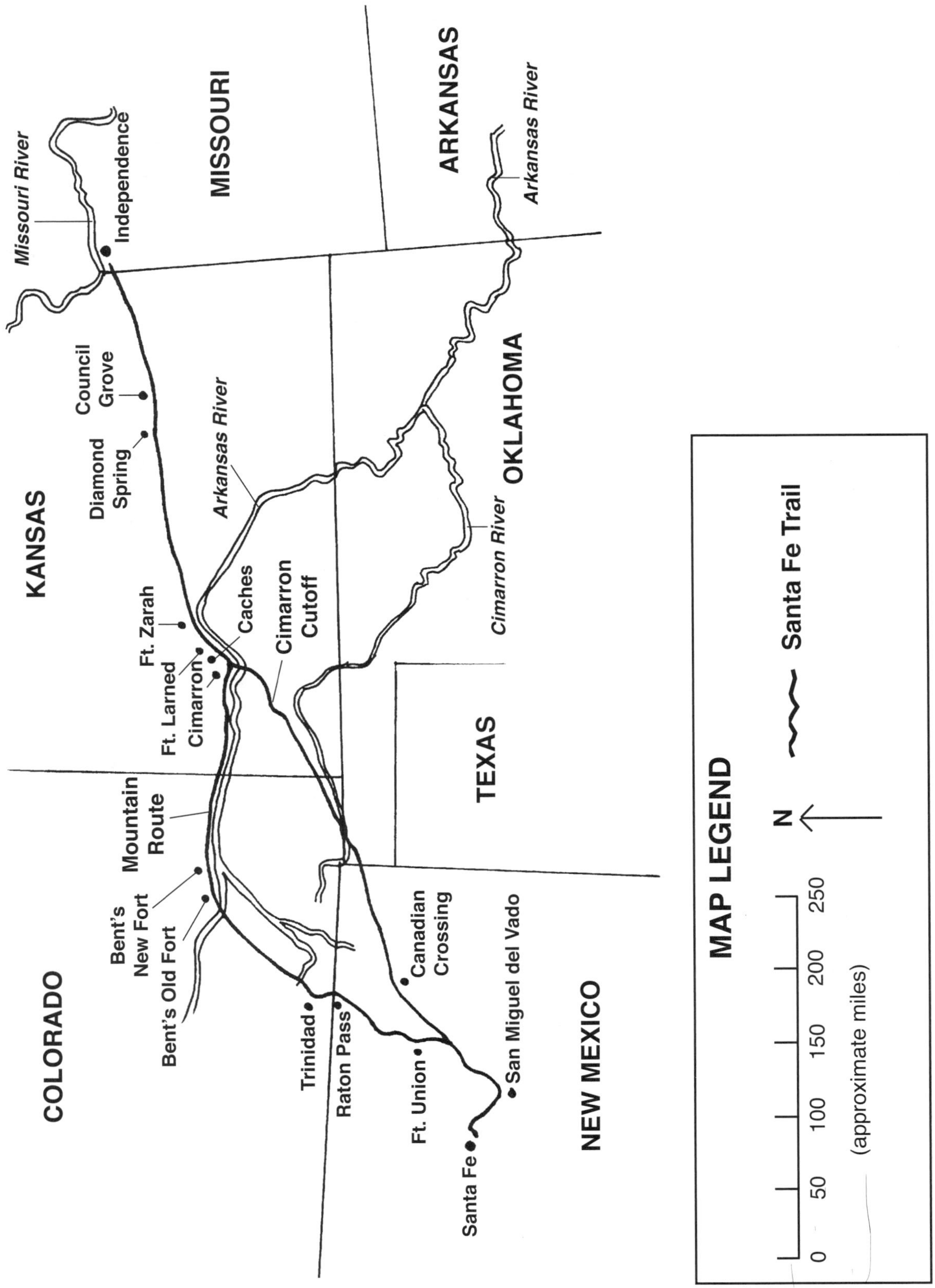

Name: ______________________ Date: ______________

Native Americans in the East

From the time the first European settlers began colonizing North America, there were conflicts with the Native Americans. What happened to the Narragansett, the Mohican, the Pokanoket, and other once-powerful groups of Native Americans? For two hundred years, the population of those and other tribes dwindled due to conflict and diseases introduced by Europeans. As white settlers pushed westward, this trend continued.

One of the few tribes to coexist with the settlers for any length of time were the Cherokee. Many Cherokee lived in northern Georgia. In 1828, when Andrew Jackson was elected president, gold was discovered at Dahlonega, Georgia. Gold fever swept the South, and the Cherokee people were attacked, their lands taken, and treaties broken.

When the Cherokee tried to use the legal system to protect their rights, the governor of Georgia stated, "Treaties were expedients by which ignorant, intractable, and savage people were induced without bloodshed to yield up what civilized peoples had a right to possess."

President Jackson was not sympathetic to Native Americans. When the Supreme Court ordered the federal government to protect the Cherokee nation from attack, Jackson refused to send help. He believed the Indian Removal Plan was the only solution to all conflicts between whites and Native Americans. This plan involved resettling all Native Americans who lived east of the Mississippi River to land west of the river.

Some members of the Cherokee nation wanted to fight this plan in court. Others wanted to go to war. Some made plans to hide in caves in the hills. Others simply gave up and moved west.

Before the plan became a law, the state of Georgia organized a lottery to give away the Cherokee land to the winners.

1. What did the Georgia governor's statement about treaties mean? ______________________

____

____

2. What do you think of the Indian Removal Plan? ______________________

____

____

3. What were the four main possible responses of the Cherokee to the Indian Removal Plan?

____

____

____

____

Name: ______________________________ Date: ______________________

The Trail of Tears

Under Andrew Jackson, the Indian Removal Act of 1830 became law. This affected all Native Americans east of the Mississippi, not only the Cherokee.

In the winter of 1831, the forced removal of the Choctaw began. The government had agreed to feed and clothe the people during their journey, but the money was never spent on provisions for them. Many were barefoot; most had no coats or blankets, yet they were forced to travel on foot across the frozen Mississippi River.

The Creeks were put in chains and forced from their homes in 1836 by U.S. soldiers. About 3,500 died of hunger and exposure before they reached their new territory. The following year, the Chickasaw were also forced to leave their homes.

A long court battle delayed their removal but did not help the Cherokee. In 1838, their nightmare began. An army of 7,000 men dragged the people from their homes without warning and herded them into camps with nothing but the clothes they wore.

An estimated 17,000 Cherokee men, women, and children began the forced relocation to what was called Indian Territory. This would later become the state of Oklahoma. The journey came to be called the Trail of Tears. About 25 percent of those who started died along the way. It took nearly six months for those who lived to reach their destination.

Of the five major tribes east of the Mississippi, only the Seminoles tried to fight. After a long, bloody war, they too were defeated and forced to move.

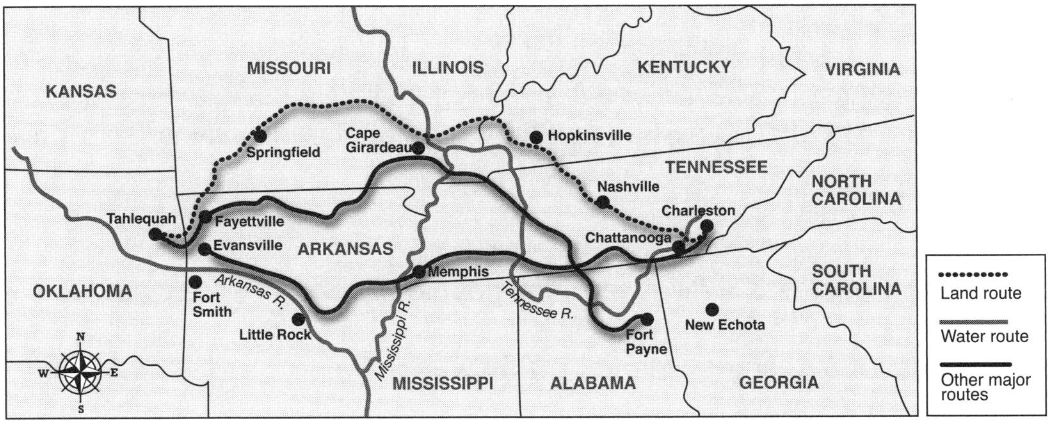

1. Why do you think the journey was later called the Trail of Tears?

____

____

____

2. Use reference sources to learn more about one of the following tribes: Creeks, Cherokees, Choctaws, Chickasaws, or Seminoles. On your own paper, describe where they lived, their lifestyles, their experiences during the forced relocations, and what happened when they arrived at their new homes.

Name: ______________________ Date: ______________

Oregon Fever

In the 1820s, mountain men and fur trappers were the first to use the route that became the Oregon Trail. Missionaries began traveling to Oregon in the 1830s. Their letters home told of the fertile land, beautiful valleys, and gentle climate of Oregon, a land where anyone who farmed would prosper.

In 1843, a provisional government drafted Oregon's first constitution called the Organic Act and established laws for claiming land. Married couples could claim up to 640 acres at no cost if they cultivated the land and lived on it for four years. Half of the land would be in the woman's name. This was a change from laws in most states where women were not allowed to own property.

When word of free land spread east, thousands were infected with "Oregon Fever," a burning desire to own and farm fertile farmland. Land was the single most important reason why people undertook the long, difficult journey along the Oregon Trail. The first large wagon train set off for Oregon in 1843 led by Jesse Applegate. The train included 120 wagons, 1,000 people, and 5,000 cattle, plus chickens, pigs, and dogs.

After 1850, the amount of free land available per couple was reduced to 320 acres. A single person could claim 160 acres. In 1854, the price of land was set at $1.25 an acre, with a limit of 320 acres for any one claim.

The Homestead Act of 1862 allowed the head of a family or single person over 21 to claim 160 acres of public land by paying a $34 fee if they lived on it and cultivated it for five years.

Circle *T* for true or *F* for False.

1. T F Oregon Fever was a disease many people caught after they arrived in Oregon.
2. T F The cost of 320 acres of land in 1854 was $400.
3. T F Women in every state were allowed to own property.
4. T F Missionaries were the first to travel the Oregon Trail.
5. T F In 1843, the law allowed married couples to claim up to 1,640 acres of free land.
6. T F Today, anyone willing to travel from Missouri to Oregon by wagon train can still claim free land.
7. T F The Organic Act stated that no pesticides could be used on farmland in Oregon.

Name: ______________________________ Date: ____________________

From Missouri to Oregon

Parts of the Oregon Trail had been blazed by Canadian explorers and the Lewis and Clark Expedition. Later, mountain men like Jim Bridger contributed their knowledge of the route and often acted as guides for groups heading west.

Oregon City was founded on the Willamette River by fur traders in 1829 and was a bustling town by 1867, the time of this photo.

The Oregon Trail was the route pioneers took from Independence, Missouri, to the Columbia River in Oregon. At first, Oregon City was their destination. Later, settlers continued south to the fertile land of the Willamette Valley.

Part of the route followed the Platte River for about 540 miles through Nebraska to Fort Laramie. The trail continued along the North Platte and Sweetwater Rivers to South Pass.

From there, settlers traveled south to Fort Bridger, Wyoming, before turning into the Bear River Valley. There they headed north to Fort Hall in Idaho.

Once in Oregon, settlers passed through the Rhonda River Valley, crossed another mountain range, and then continued on to the Columbia River.

Use the map of the Oregon Trail on page 15 and other reference sources to complete this page.

1. What does "blaze a trail" mean? ______________________________

   ____

2. In what state is Fort Laramie located? ______________________________
3. South Pass is in what range of the Rocky Mountains? ______________________________
4. In Idaho, settlers followed another river to Salmon Falls before heading north to Fort Boise. What was the name of that river?

   ____

5. What mountains did settlers cross in Oregon before they reached the Columbia River?

   ____

6. Use a modern road map. On your own paper, write directions a motorist could use to travel today from Independence, Missouri, to Oregon City, Oregon. Include the specific highways to take, total driving distance, and driving time. Calculate driving time by dividing the total miles by 50 (using 50 miles per hour as an average.)

Name: ______________________ Date: ______________

Along the Oregon Trail

According to an official government survey, the main branch of the Oregon Trail from Independence, Missouri, to Oregon City, Oregon, was 1,930 miles long. Between 1840 and 1860, about 53,000 settlers traveled the Oregon Trail.

There were many cutoffs and alternate routes along the way that people sometimes took. Some routes were shorter, but they were often more dangerous.

Use the map of the Oregon Trail on the next page to complete this activity.

1. Trace the Oregon Trail in blue on the map.
2. Besides Missouri and Oregon, what states did travelers on the Oregon Trail pass through?

   ____

   ____

Name the state along the Oregon Trail where each place is located.

Chimney Rock

3. Fort Bridger ______________
4. Willamette Valley ______________
5. Ogallala ______________
6. Chimney Rock ______________
7. Fort Laramie ______________
8. Fort Hall ______________
9. Fort Kearny ______________
10. South Pass ______________
11. Independence ______________
12. American Falls ______________
13. Soda Springs ______________
14. Oregon City ______________
15. Fort Boise ______________

Name: ______________________________ Date: ____________________

Along the Oregon Trail Map

Use this map of the Oregon Trail to complete the activities on pages 13, 14, 16, and 42.

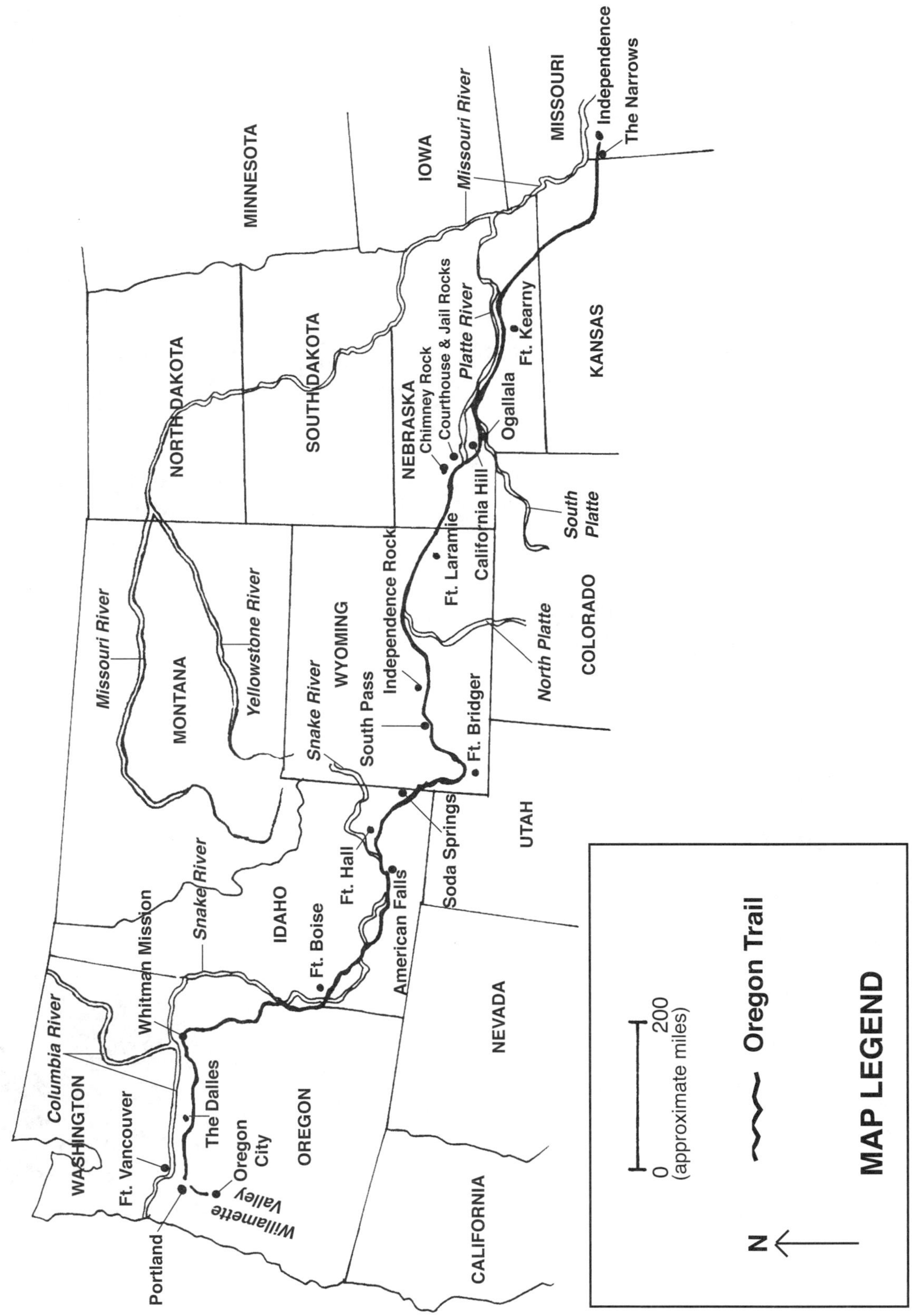

Name: ______________________________ Date: ____________________

Getting From Here to There

Use the maps of the Santa Fe and Oregon Trails on pages 9 and 15 to complete this activity.

Number the places along the Santa Fe Trail in order from east to west (1 being the farthest east and 9 being the farthest west).

_____ A. Diamond Spring

_____ B. Caches

_____ C. Raton Pass

_____ D. Fort Zarah

_____ E. Council Grove

_____ F. Fort Larned

_____ G. San Miguel del Vado

_____ H. Fort Union

_____ I. Bent's New Fort

San Miguel del Vado

Number the places along the Oregon Trail in order from east to west (1 being the farthest east and 10 being the farthest west).

_____ J. Independence Rock

_____ K. Soda Springs

_____ L. The Dalles

_____ M. Fort Kearny

_____ N. Fort Bridger

_____ O. The Narrows

_____ P. Fort Vancouver

_____ Q. Fort Boise

_____ R. Fort Hall

_____ S. Fort Laramie

Independence Rock

Name: ______________________________ Date: ______________________

In Search of Religious Freedom

Joseph Smith

Although the U.S. Constitution guarantees freedom of religion, members of the Church of Jesus Christ of Latter-day Saints were repeatedly denied that freedom.

The history of the church began in New York. Joseph Smith, the founder of the group, said that an angel had told him where to find a book written on thin gold plates by the prophet Mormon. He translated the writings that became *The Book of Mormon*, the basis for the new religion. At the time, others called the members of the church Mormons, but the Church of Jesus Christ of Latter-day Saints discourages that term today.

As membership in the church grew, nonmembers became very hostile to Smith and his followers. The members of the church moved from western New York to Ohio, to Missouri, and then to Illinois in an attempt to be allowed to practice their religion in peace. Each time they established a settlement, they gained new converts; however, they also gained new enemies and were violently expelled by angry neighbors.

In Illinois, the Latter-day Saints founded the city of Nauvoo and began building a great temple. They also began practicing **polygamy**, which Smith said was God's will. (Today the Church of Jesus Christ of Latter-day Saints is not affiliated with polygamist groups.)

Nauvoo Temple

Public outrage against polygamy was only one reason why Latter-day Saints were persecuted. People resented the church members' tendency to patronize only businesses owned by other Latter-day Saints. When Latter-day Saints voted, they all tended to vote for the same person. They also began a system of communal ownership of property that allowed church leaders to redistribute property to those in need.

When Smith announced he was running for president in 1844, he and his brother were arrested and murdered. His followers were threatened: if they stayed, they, too, would be killed.

1. Using a dictionary, define *polygamy*. ______________________________

____

2. In which states did the Latter-day Saints build settlements before Joseph Smith was killed?

____

3. What were some of the reasons why nonmembers persecuted the Latter-day Saints?

____

____

____

____

Name: ______________________________ Date: ____________________

The Latter-day Saints Move West

After Joseph Smith was killed, Brigham Young, one of Smith's 12 key followers known as apostles, became the new leader of the Church of Jesus Christ of Latter-day Saints. Young decided the members of the church would move to the area around the Great Salt Lake because there were no other settlers nearby. He began plans for the move by instructing people to grow extra crops, to store food, and to build wagons.

In February 1846, the Latter-day Saints began leaving Nauvoo. By May, thousands were spread out across hundreds of miles of prairie. Those who went ahead set up camps and planted crops for those who followed. They spent the first winter near what is now Omaha, Nebraska. Many died that winter, but the survivors did not give up.

***Crossing the Mississippi on the Ice,* painting by C.C.A. Christensen**

In the spring of 1847, Young led an advance party of 25 wagons to the valley of the Great Salt Lake. Two days after they arrived, men began planting crops to ensure there would be food for the others when they arrived. Young returned to join the main group and to lead them to their new home.

The route they followed from Illinois, across Iowa, and to the west to the Great Salt Lake became known as the Mormon Trail. Much of the trail across Nebraska and Wyoming followed the same route as the Oregon Trail. The Mormon Trail turned south toward the Great Salt Lake after leaving Fort Bridger.

Besides being a strong religious leader, Brigham Young also had great organizational skills, which were essential in coordinating the move of thousands of people from Illinois to Utah. He also made arrangements for temporary quarters in Missouri for other converts from the United States and England who would later join them in Utah.

1. List five problems Brigham Young had to deal with when thousands of members of the church left Illinois to travel west.

   ____

   ____

   ____

   ____

2. Young and other leaders planned the layout for Salt Lake City, which grew to a population of over 12,000 in four years. List five important things that would have needed to have been done to turn a barren stretch of land into a large city.

   ____

   ____

   ____

   ____

Name: ______________________ Date: ______________________

Along the Mormon Trail Map

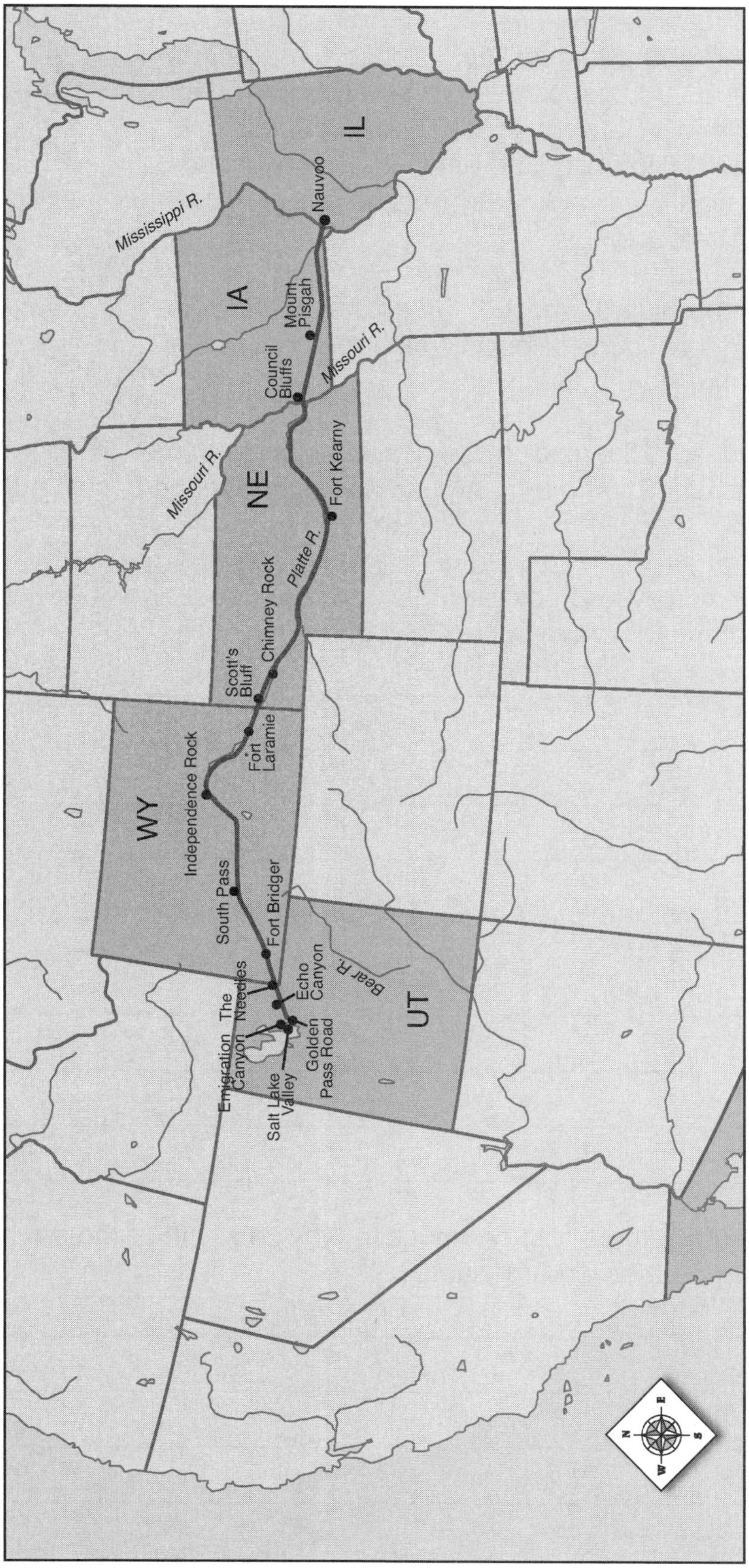

Name: ______________________ Date: ______________________

The Forty-Niners

News of gold found at Sutter's Mill and other places in California caused one of the largest and wildest migrations in history. In April 1849, 20,000 people set out in wagon trains for the gold fields of California. Between 75,000 and 100,000 people made their way to the California gold fields in 1849. Thousands more followed in the next few years. Many rode horses or mules. Some walked most of the way

Nicknamed "forty-niners," most of the gold seekers were men. By 1850, women accounted for only eight percent of the population of California.

Those who rushed to the gold fields of California were also called the "Argonauts of '49." The term Argonauts referred to the people from Greek mythology who sailed on the ship *Argo*.

1. James Marshall discovered gold at Sutter's Mill in January of 1848. Why did it take until 1849 for most of the miners to get to California?

____

____

____

____

2. Use reference sources to find the name of the leader of the mythical Argonauts and what they were searching for.

____

____

____

____

3. Read about the adventures of the Argonauts. Why do you think those who went to California in search of gold were called Argonauts?

____

____

____

____

4. On your own paper, draw a cartoon showing the forty-niners heading to California.

Name: ______________________ Date: ______________

Travel to the Gold Fields

The migration to the gold fields of California resulted in nearly 100,000 people arriving in 1849. Many thousands more followed in the next few years. There were three main modes of transportation to California.

Wagon Train

In April of 1849, 20,000 people set out in wagon trains for the gold fields of California. Most trails to the West began at Independence or St. Joseph, Missouri, or Council Bluffs, Iowa. There was never one single trail to California but rather several major routes with variations. The Oregon Trail, Santa Fe Trail, and California Trail were the three most commonly used.

Those traveling with wagon trains had to take routes that were not the most direct because of several natural obstacles: the canyons of Colorado, the Sierra Nevada Mountains, and the deserts around the Great Salt Lake. The journey by wagon train took about four to five months.

Stagecoach

Between 1850 and 1900, stagecoaches carried tens of thousands of passengers on regularly-scheduled routes across the West. Many prospective miners chose this method of travel because it was much quicker than traveling with a wagon train. Compared to modern transportation, however, a stagecoach trip was painfully uncomfortable and dreadfully slow. The trip from Missouri to California took about a month and cost $200.

Clipper Ship

Many prospectors decided to reach California by booking passage on fast clipper ships. The trip around Cape Horn was long, dangerous, and expensive. This journey took about 100 days if everything went well. Strong currents, icebergs, and fierce winds off Cape Horn often caused ships to go off course, adding more time to the journey.

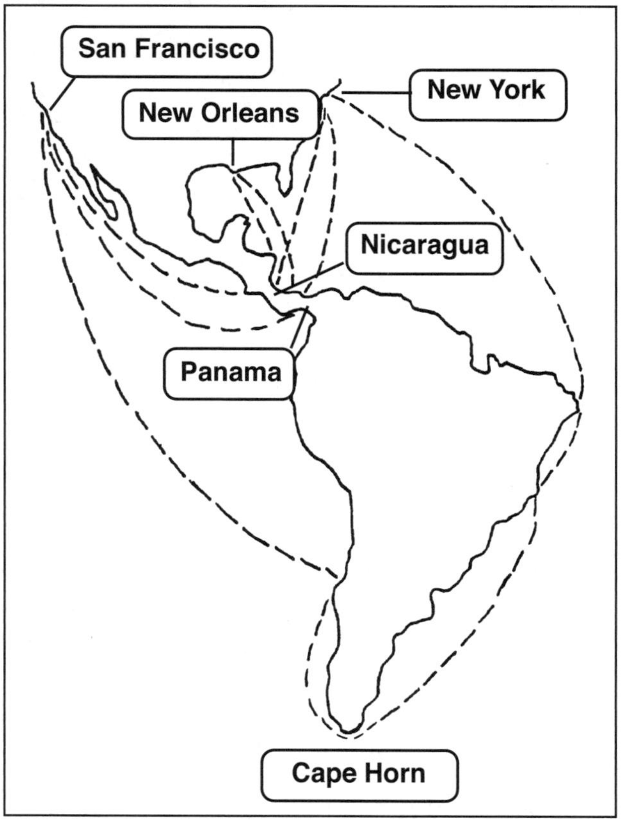

Greedy ship captains signed up as many passengers as they could crowd onto a ship. People often slept three to a bed. The supply of ships did not nearly meet the demand for travel, and many older ships that were barely seaworthy were brought into service. Once ships reached California, the crews often deserted to join the Gold Rush. Ships were abandoned and left to rot.

A second option was to sail across the Gulf of Mexico to Panama. From there, travelers walked or rode horses 100 miles through dense jungles to Panama City in the hopes of catching a ship heading north on the Pacific side. This route was also uncertain, long, and dangerous. The food was terrible, and the water was thick, murky, and often filled with insects. Yellow fever, malaria, dysentery, and cholera prevented many prospective miners from reaching California.

Name: ______________________ Date: ______________________

Along the California Trail Map

Use the map below and the information from page 21 to complete the questions.

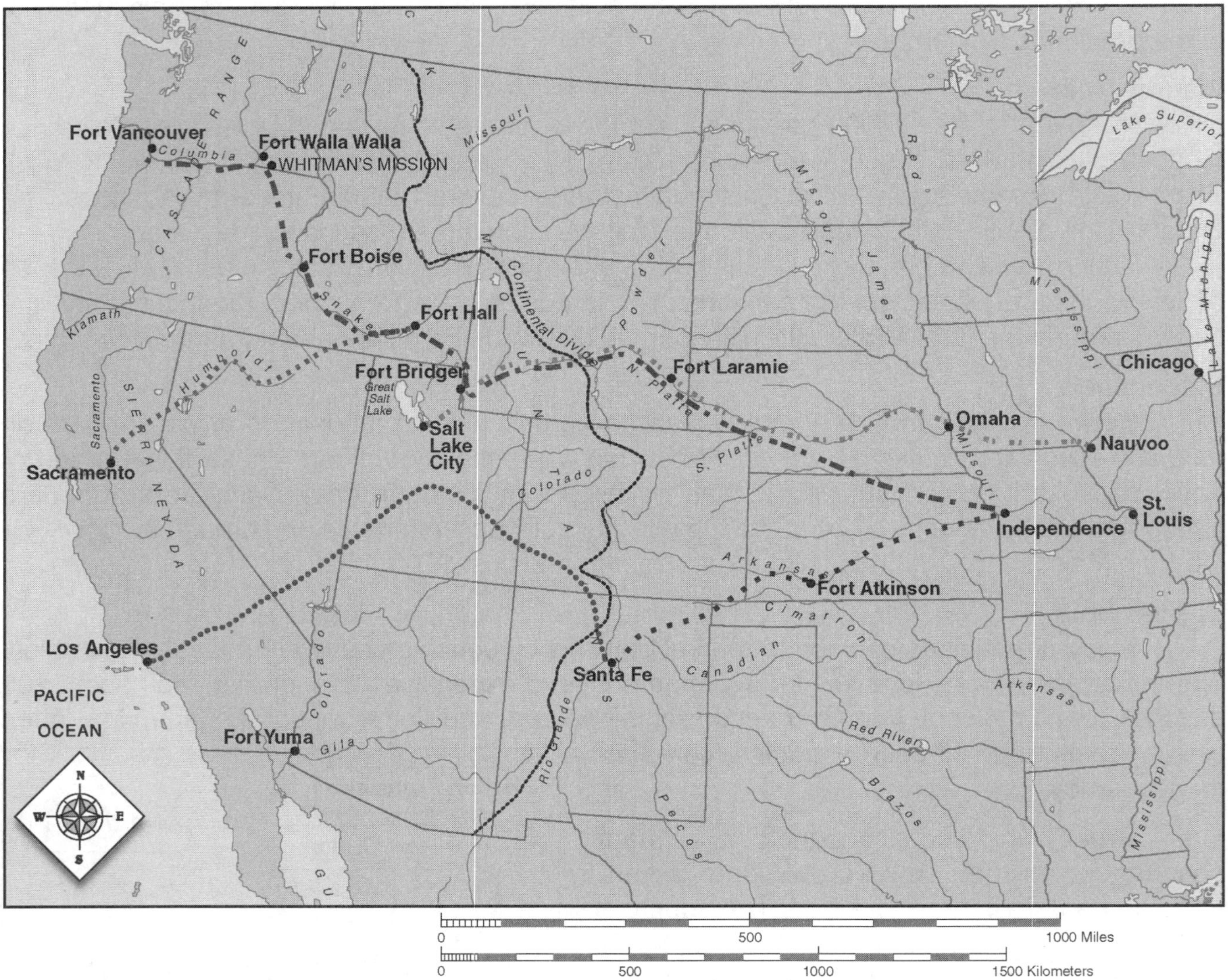

1. Which two trails ended in California? ______________________

   ____

2. Using the map scale, approximately how many miles was the journey from Independence, Missouri, along the Oregon and California Trails to Sacramento, California?

   ____

3. About how long did each route to the gold fields take if all went well?

   Wagon train: __________ Stagecoach: __________ Clipper ship: __________

Name: ______________________________ Date: ______________________

Decisions, Decisions

Imagine traveling cross-country in a minivan with your family, pets, and all your possessions. What would you take? What would you leave behind? How long would the trip take?

What if that minivan were actually a large, sturdy wagon with high sides, there were no roads, and your top speed was 15 to 20 miles a day?

1. Think of a place that's about 20 miles from where you live. How long does it usualy take you to get there?

   ____

Van, pickup, or car? When people buy vehicles, they choose between different styles, features, accessories, and engines. They consider price and the reason they need a vehicle. The pioneers also had to decide how to travel. Many types of wagons were available, but the Conestoga was considered the best and was the most expensive. Pioneers also had to decide on the type of "engines" for their covered wagons: horses, oxen, or mules.

2. Use reference sources to find advantages and disadvantages of these three types of animals: (A) horses, (B) oxen, and (C) mules. Consider cost, strength, and "fuel" (feed).

	Advantages	Disadvantages
A. Horses	________________	________________
	________________	________________
	________________	________________
	________________	________________
B. Oxen	________________	________________
	________________	________________
	________________	________________
	________________	________________
C. Mules	________________	________________
	________________	________________
	________________	________________
	________________	________________

Name: ______________________ Date: ______________________

Conestoga Wagons

Conestoga wagons were originally developed for hauling freight on the east coast. They were sturdy, well-built wagons that were often used for traveling along the Santa Fe or Oregon Trail. The strong, broad wheels allowed the wagons to cross rutted roads, muddy flats, and the non-roads of the prairie. The curved floor was designed to reduce load shifting. Conestogas were capable of carrying loads up to six tons!

Besides Conestogas, settlers also used common farm wagons with canvas tops supported by wooden arches. Although not as sturdy as Conestogas, these wagons were lighter and easier to pull.

The white-topped wagons were nicknamed "prairie schooners" because their high, white canvas tops looked like sailing ships as they crossed the sea of grass on the American prairie.

1. Use reference sources. Why were they called "Conestoga" wagons?

____

____

2. Write a slogan or jingle a salesperson of Conestoga wagons might have used.

Example: If you plan to travel west,
Conestogas are the best.

____

____

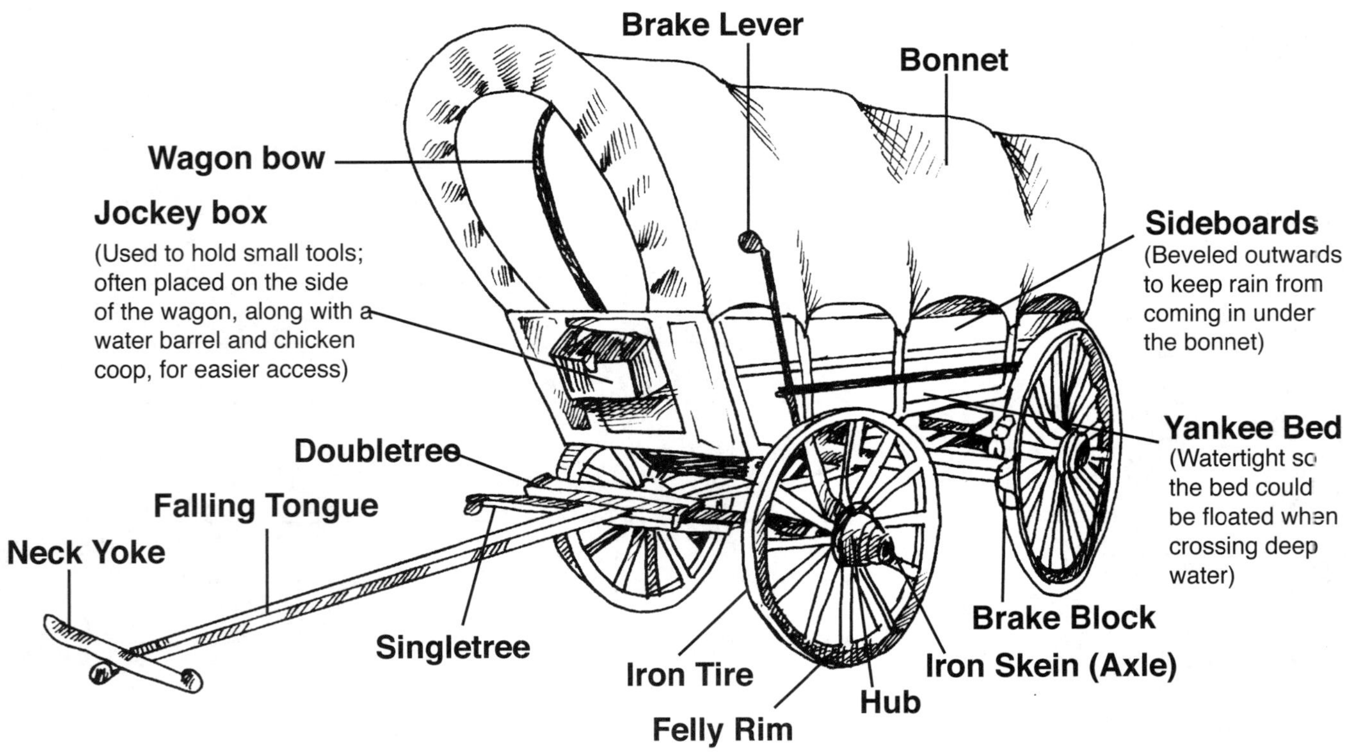

Name: ______________________________ Date: ____________________

Supplying the Wagons

The pioneers couldn't stop at malls or convenience stores along the way. Although some places along the trail did carry supplies, the prices were higher and the availability of items was uncertain.

The typical covered wagon was four feet across and ten to 12 feet long. Much of that space was filled with food. Because of the amount of energy used, people needed nearly twice the amount of food per day they would normally eat. The following is what was recommended for one adult to make the journey to Oregon.

200 lbs. flour
10 lbs. rice
25 lbs. sugar
30 lbs. flat crackerlike bread
10 lbs. salt
5 lbs. coffee
$\frac{1}{2}$ bushel dried beans
75 lbs. bacon
2 lbs. baking soda
1 bushel dried fruit
$\frac{1}{2}$ bushel corn meal

Pioneers took cattle and other livestock with them. They could make butter from cow's milk and get eggs from chickens.

Berries or edible roots could be gathered along the way. Hunters sometimes found small game and occasionally shot larger animals, like bison or deer. When they were desperate, they ate snakes and prairie dogs. For the most part, the pioneers ate biscuits and beans, three times a day, day after day after day!

1. How would you feel about eating this way for several months? ____________________

2. What foods that you normally eat would you miss most? ____________________

3. The pioneers also had to bring everything they needed to start a new home and begin farming when they arrived. Besides food, water, and clothing, what else do you think the pioneers took with them?

Name: ______________________ Date: ______________

The Cost of Supplies

The cost of supplies varied from month to month and town to town. These prices would have been typical in Missouri in the 1840s and 1850s.

ITEM	PRICE	ITEM	PRICE
ox	$30–35	milk cow	$70–75
mule	$10–15	horse	$25–75
nails	$0.07/lb.	soap	$0.15/lb.
coffee pot	$0.75	candles	$0.15/lb.
washtub	$1.25	rifle	$15
shotgun	$10	hunting knife	$1
flour	$0.02/lb.	corn meal	$0.05/lb.
bacon	$0.05/lb.	sugar	$0.04/lb.
coffee	$0.10/lb.	salt	$0.06/lb.
pepper	$0.08/lb.	vinegar	$0.25/gal.
tea	$0.60/lb.	rice	$0.05/lb.
beans	$0.06/pound	dried fruit	$0.06/lb.

1. Four to six oxen were needed to pull a heavy wagon. What is the least it would have cost for six oxen? ______________
2. Which would have cost more: four oxen or eight mules? ______________
3. How much would it have cost to buy a coffee pot, a washtub, ten pounds of soap, ten pounds of candles, a rifle, and a hunting knife? ______________
4. How much would it have cost for 75 pounds of bacon, 25 pounds of sugar, five pounds of coffee, ten pounds of salt, and ten pounds of rice? ______________
5. Which cost more: ten pounds of beans or two gallons of vinegar? ______________
6. How much more per pound did tea cost than coffee? ______________
7. In Oregon, nails sold for 17 cents a pound. Why do you think nails were more expensive in Oregon than in Missouri? ______________

____

8. Compare the prices of any three food items then and now.

Item	**Cost Then**	**Cost Now**	**Difference**

Name: ______________________________ Date: ______________________

Joining a Wagon Train

Rather than facing the perils of a long journey alone, most people who traveled west joined a wagon train—a group of ten or more wagons with 50 or more people led by a guide.

During the journey, the people in a wagon train were like a small community. They elected leaders and made their own laws. What kinds of laws do you think people needed during a hazardous journey of four to six months?

Most wagon trains left in early May. Timing was critical for the long journey. If they left too early in the year, there might not be enough grass to feed the animals along the way, and the ground might be too soggy. If they left too late, summer drought may have killed the grass before they could cross the prairie. They could encounter blizzards by the time they tried to cross the mountains.

Water was critical for people and animals, but not much could be carried because of the weight. Finding water along the way could make the difference between life and death.

1. What advantages would there be in traveling in a group? (Consider breakdowns, food gathering, medical problems, and other dangers.)

____

____

____

____

2. Write three laws you think would be most important and the reasons for each.

____

____

____

____

____

____

3. Besides being used for drinking, why else was water needed?

____

____

____

____

Name: ______________________ Date: ______________________

Traveling With a Wagon Train

When a family joined a wagon train heading west, they knew they were undertaking a long, dangerous journey. For a time, their wagons became their homes. Since the wagons were packed from top to bottom with supplies, there was very little living space. Many travelers slept under their wagons unless it was too wet or cold.

As the groups traveled west, wagon trains stretched out for a half-mile or more. The best position for a wagon was near the front of the column. Those in the rear had to "eat dust" all day long. In most wagon trains, people changed places in line each day.

On the trail, the day began before dawn. There were chores to do, breakfast to make and eat, and animals to feed, water, and harness. The travelers needed to leave early to travel as many miles as possible while there was still daylight. Wagon trains averaged 12 to 15 miles a day, depending on the terrain, the weather, and other factors.

Wagons forming a night circle

Each wagon had to be in its assigned place when the leader gave the command to start. He might blow a bugle or shout the words, "Wagons, ho!" Those not ready to leave on time lost their assigned places and went to the back of the line. Being at the front of the wagon train was an advantage because it was less dusty, but it also meant those who were first in line had to be ready to roll earlier than the others.

Wagon trains halted before dark. They turned the wagons to form a tight ring called a "night circle" as protection against attack. Men took turns as sentries around the outside of the circle. Inside the circle, people cooked, washed clothes, took care of their animals, made repairs to their wagons, and visited with each other. Besides being a form of protection, the night circle also gave the people on the wagon train a sense of community.

1. What do you think the phrase "eat dust" means? ______________________

____

____

2. What other disadvantages could there be for those at the front of the wagon train?

____

____

____

____

3. On your own paper, explain what "a sense of community" means to you. Why would it have been important to those traveling with a wagon train?

Name: ____________________________ Date: ____________________

Perils Along the Way

Weather often caused problems on the trail. Extreme heat caused sunburn or sunstroke. Streams dried up when it was hot. Cold caused frostbite.

For each type of weather listed, write some potential problems that could result.

1. Thunderstorm ____
____
2. Lightning ____
____
3. Blizzard ____
____
4. Tornado ____
____
5. Heat ____
____
6. Dust storm ____
____

Mosquitoes could be very annoying, but other types of animals the pioneers encountered on the trails could cause bigger problems.

7. List two animals and reasons why they could be hazardous to travelers.
____
____
____
____

8. Imagine you are a pioneer heading west along the Santa Fe Trail. It's early morning on a hot, windy day. The temperature is already over 90 degrees. The wind blows the dust constantly across the prairie, getting inside everything. You're sweaty and dirty. The water barrel is almost empty. You must keep going to reach water before nightfall. On your own paper, describe your day in as much detail as possible.

Name: ________________________ Date: ________________

Obstacles Along the Trail

1. Crossing wide or deep rivers with wagons and livestock was difficult and dangerous. Use reference sources to find out how pioneers made these crossings.

2. Crossing mountains was another peril the pioneers faced. Going up the mountain could be as difficult and dangerous as going down.

   Why do you think going up a mountain would be difficult and dangerous?

3. Why do you think going down a mountain would be a problem?

4. Cliffs and river banks could also present obstacles. Look at the illustration to see how they moved the wagon up the bank.

   The illustration shows how they moved a wagon up a steep bank, but how do you think they got the animals to the top?

Name: ______________________ Date: ______________

What Was Essential?

1. Circle the 20 items you think would be the most important for pioneers to take along with them in their wagons.

Ax	Coffee	Knives	Needles & thread	Soap
Baking soda	Coffee pot	Lantern & oil	Pen & ink	Spare wagon wheel
Bible	Corn meal	Lard	Piano	Spinning wheel
Blankets	Dried beans	Large-brimmed hats	Razor	Sugar
Books	Dried fruit		Rice	Table
Boots	Firewood	Large soup kettle	Rifle	Tea
Butter	Flour	Long underwear	Salt	Tents
Butter churn	Frying pan	Matches	Salt pork	Vegetable seeds
Candles	Gloves	Medicines	Shoes	Washtub
Chairs	Hammer	Molasses	Shovel	Whetstone
Chickens	Hatchet	Nails	Silk dresses	Wool socks
				Writing paper

2. List the 20 items you circled in the order you think would be most important (1) to least important (20).

1. ______________ 11. ______________
2. ______________ 12. ______________
3. ______________ 13. ______________
4. ______________ 14. ______________
5. ______________ 15. ______________
6. ______________ 16. ______________
7. ______________ 17. ______________
8. ______________ 18. ______________
9. ______________ 19. ______________
10. ______________ 20. ______________

3. Give reasons for the three items you chose as the most important.

____
____
____
____

Name: ______________________________ Date: ______________________

Take It or Leave It?

Pioneers had to make many difficult decisions along the trail. Sometimes they had to abandon items they had brought from home. The decisions on what to take and what to abandon could be very difficult, but they could also be a matter of life or death.

For each pair of items, decide which you should abandon and which you should keep. Explain your reasons for each.

1. An empty water barrel or a beautiful dresser your grandfather made for you when you were a child?

   Abandon ____________________ because ______________________________

   Keep ____________________ because ______________________________

2. A keg of nails for building your new home or a barrel of flour?

   Abandon ____________________ because ______________________________

   Keep ____________________ because ______________________________

3. A spinning wheel or two barrels of salt pork?

   Abandon ____________________ because ______________________________

   Keep ____________________ because ______________________________

4. A cookstove or the baby's cradle?

   Abandon ____________________ because ______________________________

   Keep ____________________ because ______________________________

5. A barrel of flour or a box of school books?

   Abandon ____________________ because ______________________________

   Keep ____________________ because ______________________________

6. A beautiful wooden trunk filled with blankets and quilts or a hand-carved maple headboard and bedframe?

   Abandon ____________________ because ______________________________

   Keep ____________________ because ______________________________

Name: ______________________ Date: ______________________

What Is It?

Use reference sources to identify each item pioneers may have taken with them on their journey to the west. Briefly explain what the item was used for.

Example: Butter churn: Used to make butter.

Use the words in the box as clues. Not all words will be used.

butter churn	horse collar	horseshoe	wheel rim
mule collar	ox yoke	razor strop	whetstone
spinning wheel	wagon jack	wheel chock	wooden barrel

1. ______________________
2. ______________________
3. ______________________
4. ______________________
5. ______________________
6. ______________________
7. ______________________
8. ______________________

1.

2.
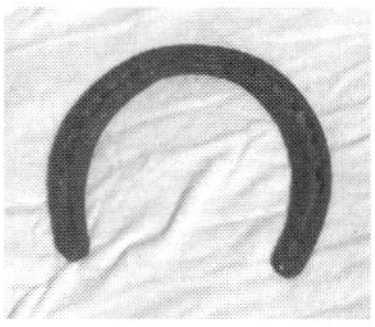

3.
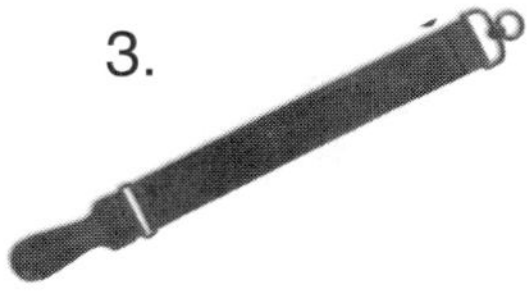

4.
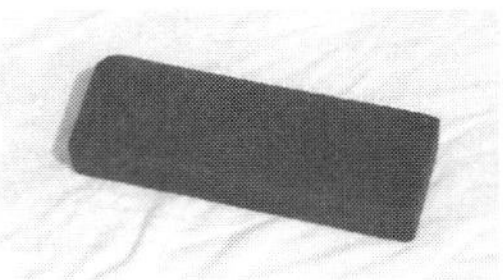

5.
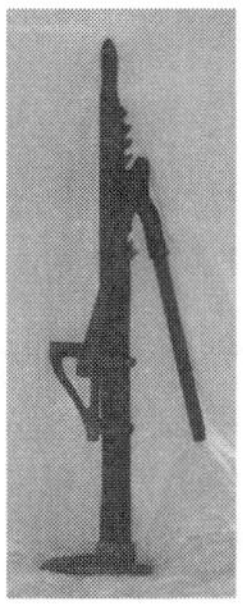

6.
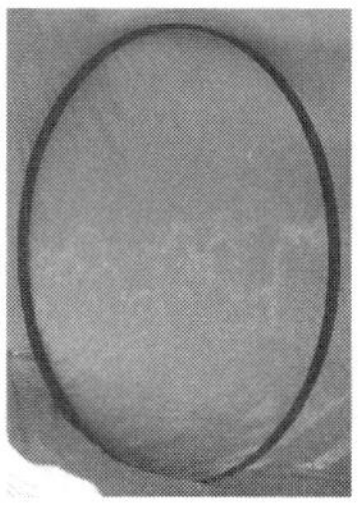

7.

8.

Name: ______________________________ Date: ____________________

Children On the Trail

Most children traveled the western trails with their families. When parents died along the trail, children were usually adopted by another family and continued the journey. At times, orphans might be left with families at forts, missions, or small settlements along the way. Migrants heading west on the Oregon Trail reportedly had an average of 3.4 children with them.

Although they didn't attend school while on the trail, the four-and-a-half to six-month journey was far from a vacation. Many children kept a diary or read the Bible to practice their reading and writing skills.

Except during very bad weather, only the very sick, very young, or very old rode in covered wagons. Many children walked a good part of the journey to lighten the load for the animals.

Riding in a wagon wasn't very comfortable, and children found that walking helped keep them from being bored. As they walked, they searched for berries and other edible plants and picked up firewood or bison chips for fuel. Dried bison chips burned much more quickly than wood. It took two to three bushels of bison chips to cook a meal.

Even very young children had chores to do. The older the child, the more work was expected. Chores included tending the livestock, fetching water, taking care of younger children, helping with the cooking, washing clothes, and fishing.

Most children were so busy with chores and traveling that they had little time to play. However, they did participate in singing and dancing at night around the campfire, visited friends, and played games like Leapfrog, Hide the Thimble, Nine Men's Morris, and Crack-the-Whip.

1. How would you feel about walking most of the way on a 1,000- to 2,000-mile trip?

____

____

____

____

2. What kinds of games could you and your friends play without fancy toys and equipment?

____

____

____

____

Name: ______________________________ Date: ______________________

Journal of a Pioneer

John Bidwell, a member of the first wagon train to head west in 1841, wrote an account of the six-month journey from Missouri.

Pioneer Journal

"The party consisted of sixty-nine, including men, women, and children. We had no cows ... and the lack of milk was a great deprivation to the children. My gun was an old flint-lock rifle, but a good one."

When the group was ready to start, they realized that "... no one knew where to go, even the captain ... We knew only that California lay west, and that was the extent of our knowledge."

When their guide joined them, the group set out for Idaho. "For a time, until we reached the Platte River, one day was much like another ... We had to make the road [as we went], frequently digging down steep banks, filling gulches, removing stones, etc."

"One of our men who chanced to be out hunting ... suddenly appeared without mule, gun, or pistol, and lacking most of his clothes, and in great excitement reported that he had been surrounded by thousands of Indians."

South Platte River in Nebraska

The "thousands of Indians" turned out to be a party of about 40 Cheyennes "... who did not intend to hurt the man or take his mule or gun, but that he was so excited when he saw them that they had to disarm him to keep him from shooting them."

"On the Platte River ... we had a taste of a cyclone; first came a terrific shower, followed by a fall of hail to the depth of four inches, some of the stones being as large as turkeys' eggs; and the next day a waterspout—an angry, huge, whirling cloud column ... passed ... behind us. We stopped and braced ourselves against our wagons to keep them from being overturned. Had it struck us, it doubtless would have demolished us."

By the time they reached Idaho, one person "had accidentally shot and killed himself ... another had left us at Fort Laramie ... Three [others] turned back ... to return home."

Half of the party continued on to Oregon and the other half to California. "The days were very hot, the nights almost freezing. The first day our little company went only about ten miles ..."

They encountered "thickets so dense as to exclude the sun, and roaring little streams in deep, dark chasms ... paths which looked untrodden except by grizzly bears."

1. On another sheet of paper, make journal entries for three other events that may have occurred while a wagon train traveled west.

Name: ______________________ Date: ______________

Where the Bison Once Roamed

No story of the western trails would be complete without mention of the vast herds of bison, numbering between 30 million and 200 million animals, that once roamed the American plains.

Bull Bison With Herd

American bison, also known as North American buffalo, can weigh up to 2,000 pounds and be more than 12 feet long and over 6 feet tall at the peak of the massive shoulder hump. They are the largest land mammal in America. More than 20,000 years ago, they dominated the American plains from the Mississippi River west to the Rocky Mountains.

Native Americans hunted bison for thousands of years, killing only what they needed and using every part of the animal for food, clothing, and tools.

Travelers who crossed the great plains in the early 1800s often heard the rumbling of what sounded like thunder in the distance, even when the skies were clear. Suddenly, the ground began to shake as a huge herd of bison thundered past.

The early settlers and those who followed were responsible for the near-extinction of the bison. First came trappers and fur traders, people who made their living selling meat and hides. As railroad and telegraph crews worked their way across the plains, hunters shot bison to provide food for the workers, often taking only the best meat and leaving the rest. Later, train companies offered tourists the chance to shoot bison from the windows of their coaches. The animals they killed were left to rot in the sun. People even held bison-killing contests to see who could kill the most animals in the shortest amount of time. Buffalo Bill Cody reportedly shot more than 4,000 in two years.

Some officials thought destroying bison herds would help defeat Native Americans who resisted the takeover of their lands by white settlers. James Throckmorton, a Congressman from Texas, stated, "It would be a great step forward in the civilization of the Indians and the preservation of peace on the border if there was not a buffalo in existence."

By 1880, the extinction was nearly complete. Where millions of bison had once roamed, only a few thousand remained, and even that number continued to decline.

1. Using reference sources either in print or online, list at least five products Native Americans got or made from bison. Be specific.

   ____

   ____

   ____

   ____

2. Use reference sources to write a report about what is being done to rebuild the herds of bison that once roamed the American West.

Name: ______________________________ Date: ____________________

I Have Seen the Elephant

People who planned to travel west announced they were going "to see the elephant."

Those who went partway and turned back for any reason said they had seen "the elephant's tracks" or "the tail of the elephant."

This phrase came from a story about one of the circus parades that featured elephants. According to the story, a farmer heard the circus was in town. He had never seen an elephant and was very excited about the prospect. He loaded his wagon with vegetables to take to market, expecting to make a large profit.

On the way to town, he met the circus parade, led by an elephant. The farmer was thrilled, but his horses were terrified. They bolted, overturned the wagon, and ruined the vegetables.

"I don't give a hang," said the farmer, "for I have seen the elephant."

1. What do you think "seeing the elephant" meant to the farmer? ____________________

____

____

2. What do you think "seeing the elephant" meant to people who were traveling west?

____

____

____

3. When the first astronauts landed on the moon, they "saw the elephant." Give two examples of people who have "seen the elephant."

____

____

____

____

____

Name: ______________________________ Date: ____________________

Forts Along the Trails

Many forts along the Oregon and Santa Fe Trails were under the control of the U.S. Army. They housed soldiers who were stationed along the trails to keep peace with the Native Americans and protect travelers. However, some forts were owned by trading companies.

Forts provided places for travelers to rest, buy or trade for supplies, and to get equipment repaired. Prices for goods were usually much higher at forts than they were at the beginning of the trails.

Although the area enclosed by a fort was like a small community, the buildings were far from elegant. The buildings at Fort Bridger, built in 1843 by mountain man Jim Bridger, were "log cabins, rudely constructed," according to immigrant Edwin Bryant. Another traveler, Joel Palmer, described it as "… built of poles dabbed with mud."

Most forts were square or rectangular areas enclosed by strong wooden walls. Inside the walls were barracks for the soldiers, homes for the officers, offices, kitchens, bakeries, and mess halls. There were stables and grazing areas for the animals, vegetable gardens, and of course, latrines, since there was no indoor plumbing. Every fort needed a source of water—usually a well—for drinking, bathing, and doing laundry.

Some forts included buildings for carpenters, barbers, blacksmiths, dentists, or doctors. Some type of general store or trading center could also be found at most forts.

1. Why do you think forts were made of wood?

____

____

2. Why do you think forts weren't very elegant places?

____

____

3. What do you think it would have been like to have been a soldier stationed at a fort?

____

____

____

____

4. On another sheet of paper, design a fort to house 100 soldiers. Draw the fort and buildings to scale. Label all the buildings and open areas inside the walls. Don't forget to include the items mentioned in the text as well as any other buildings you think would have been important. Be creative and have fun.

Name: ______________________________ Date: ______________________

Native Americans in the West

Hundreds of groups of Native Americans lived in U.S. territories west of the Mississippi River from the Canadian border to Mexico and west to the Pacific coast. They had distinctive lifestyles and cultures. Eventual conflict with white settlers was about the only thing they all had in common.

Use reference sources to learn about the history of one tribe, its culture, types of homes, economic system, social system, and eventual contact with white settlers. Write a report that includes maps and illustrations.

Pacific Northwest Region

Chastacosta
Chehalis
Chimakum
Chinook
Clatskanie
Clatsop
Coast Salish
Coos
Cowlitz
Duwamish
Humptulips
Makah
Puyallup
Quileute
Quinault
Siletz
Siuslaw
Skagit
Skokomish
Snoqualmie
Tillamook
Tututni
Umpqua
Yaquina

Makah basket featuring a sea canoe woven from wrapped-twine cedar bark and grass.

Replica Native American burial canoe erected to honor Chief Comcomly of the Chinook

Southwest Region

Aravaipa Apache
Cocopah
Coyotera Apache
Halchidhoma
Havasupai
Hopi
Huzlapai
Jemez
Jicarilla Apache
Keres
Maricopa
Mimbreno
Mojave
Navajo
Pima
Quechan (Yuma)
Tewa
Tiwa
Tohono O'odham
Yavapai Apache
Zuni

Katcina figures drawn by a Native American Hopi artist. Katcinas can represent gods, spirits, ancestors, or clouds.

Typical house of the early Cocopah in Arizona

Name: ______________________________ Date: ____________________

The End of the Trail

After nearly six months of traveling, most wagon trains reached their destinations. Even those who had not met disasters along the way must have been worn out from the trip. But the hard work did not end when the journey was over.

When people arrived at the end of the trail, their work was only beginning. They needed to claim land, build homes, plant fields, or open businesses.

The oldest house in Santa Fe, showing adobe construction methods

For people arriving in Oregon, the first task was to file a claim for free land in Oregon City.

Most people who traveled to Oregon settled in the Willamette River Valley, where trees were plentiful and winters were much milder than they had been in the East.

In the Southwest, wood was too scarce to use for building homes. Instead, people built with adobe. Adobe homes stay cool during hot days and retain warmth at night.

People ate, slept, cooked, and lived in homes that were quite small by today's standards. After living in a covered wagon for several months, however, any home, even a small one, must have seemed like a luxury.

1. How would you have felt once you finally reached your destination? ____________________

____

____

____

2. Why do you think the government offered people free land? ____________________

____

____

____

3. Use reference sources. What is adobe? ____________________

____

4. Use reference sources. On your own paper, describe the steps needed to build an adobe house.

Name: ______________________________ Date: ______________________

Building Wooden Homes

In Oregon where wood was plentiful, people built log cabins or wooden frame houses. It took a lot of work to build either type of home. If people lived near a sawmill, they could buy wooden planks to build a frame house. If not, they usually built log cabins.

To build log cabins, people cut down trees, stripped off the bark, and cut the logs to the same length. Then the logs were notched on the ends so they would fit together as they were laid one on top of the other to build the walls.

Small windows and a door were cut out of the log walls. Windows were covered with glass, parchment, animal skins, or wooden shutters. Doors were made of wood or hides. The final step was to build a roof of wooden shingles and fill in the spaces between the logs with wood chips, moss, mud, or clay.

1. Before building a log cabin, a site needed to be chosen and prepared. If you were going to build a log cabin, what type of a site would you want?

____

____

____

2. What tools would people need to clear the underbrush from an area? ______________

____

3. What tools would people need to cut down trees and build a log cabin? ______________

____

4. Number these steps in order for building a log cabin from 1 (first) to 8 (last).

_____ A. Cover the roof with shingles.
_____ B. Cut logs to the same length.
_____ C. Cut down trees.
_____ D. Cut notches in the logs.
_____ E. Strip off the bark.
_____ F. Cut out a window and door.
_____ G. Fill in the spaces between the logs.
_____ H. Choose and prepare a site.

Name: ______________________________ Date: ____________________

From Pittsburgh to the Willamette Valley

Use clues in the sentences and the Oregon Trail map on page 15 to number the events in sequential order from 1 (first) to 14 (last).

_______ A. The wagon train crossed the Kansas River at Union Ferry, and then it continued on to The Narrows.

_______ B. Fifteen miles past California Hill, the wagon train reached Windlass Hill, a sharp decline, making it extremely treacherous and dangerous.

_______ C. When it left Fort Laramie, the wagon train passed Ayers Natural Bridge and Independence Rock and then traveled through South Pass on its way to Fort Bridger.

_______ D. Once it successfully made it down Windlass Hill, the wagon train continued on past Courthouse Rock and Jail Rock, famous natural landmarks.

_______ E. The wagon train camped at Soda Springs before heading to Fort Hall and then continued on to Fort Boise, where the Jacobsons bought supplies. The wagon train then crossed the Blue Mountains.

_______ F. The Jacobson family traveled by stagecoach from Pittsburgh, Pennsylvania, to Independence, Missouri.

_______ G. The Jacobsons continued on from Oregon City to the Willamette Valley.

_______ H. Past the Blue Mountains, the wagon train continued on to The Dalles and then to Fort Vancouver, the last fort on the Oregon Trail.

_______ I. From Jail Rock, the Jacobsons could see Chimney Rock, 14 miles ahead. They continued on to Fort Laramie.

_______ J. West of Fort Bridger, the wagon train had to climb the steep incline called Big Hill and continue 37 miles northwest to Soda Springs.

_______ K. Finally, the wagon train arrived in Oregon City.

_______ L. Everyone rested at Fort Kearny before attempting to cross the South Platte River and make the difficult climb up the steep California Hill.

_______ M. The Jacobsons purchased supplies and a wagon in Independence, joined a wagon train, and set off for Oregon.

_______ N. The wagons traveled single file through The Narrows between the Little Blue River and steep, rocky cliffs on their way to Fort Kearny.

Name: ______________________________ Date: ____________________

Pioneer Medicine

When pioneers got sick on the trail, there were few doctors or medicines available. Some diseases that are rare today were common then and were sometimes fatal. Even a toothache could be a major problem if there were no dentists in the area.

Since doctors were not always available on the trails to Oregon, California, and Santa Fe, pioneers had to bring and use their own medicines and remedies for everything from a cold to toothache, snakebite, bullet wounds, or malaria.

- **Aloe vera** was used to make a soothing lotion and ointment. It is still available today, usually as an ingredient in hand lotions.
- **Capsicum** was used to treat dysentery.
- Chewing **chamomile** helped relieve toothaches.
- **Epsom salts** were dissolved in water to soak sprained joints. Pioneers used **iodine** to keep wounds from becoming infected. **Ipecac** was used to induce vomiting in a person who had swallowed something poisonous. Epsom salts, iodine, and ipecac are still used today for the same purposes.
- **Witch hazel** is a solution of alcohol and the extract of the bark of the witch hazel plant that can be applied to wounds to stop bleeding.

Duffy's Elixir, Merchants Celebrated Gargling Oil for Man and Beast, and Dr. Watson's Great Invincible Stiff Joint Panacea were medicines, often called **snake-oil medicines**, used in the mid 1800s, but they had no real medicinal value. Other remedies included putting a dead spider on a string around a person's neck to reduce fever, placing a toad on a cut to reduce infections, and carrying an onion in a pocket to prevent snakebite.

Do some research to find the answers to the following questions.

1. What did pioneers use camphor for? ______________________________

   ____

2. Laudanum was a medicine made from alcohol and opium. It was very effective as a pain killer, but it had one major drawback. What was that?

   ____

3. Quinine was made from the bark of the South American cinchona tree. What disease was quinine used to prevent and treat?

   ____

4. Willow bark was used to relieve pain. The main ingredient in willow bark, salicylic acid, is also the main ingredient in what common medicine used today?

   ____

Name: ______________________________ Date: ____________________

Tidbits of Trail Trivia

- The Osage tribe gave the U.S. government permission to use the Santa Fe Trail in 1825. The council where the right-of-way was granted was held under a tree (Council Oak). For many years, Council Grove was the only trading post between Independence, Missouri, and Santa Fe, New Mexico.

- The Santa Fe Trail was heavily used during the Mexican War to transport supplies for the army.

- Over 39,000 people were recorded passing through Fort Laramie in the first half of 1849. Thousands more probably passed there without being recorded.

- In 1852, Ezra Meeker made his first wagon journey across the Oregon Trail. At the age of 76, Meeker loaded up a wagon, hitched up two oxen, and made the trip again. Even though the oxen died along the way, Meeker enjoyed the trip so much, he did it again when he was in his 80s. He made the same trip several more times by train, car, and airplane.

- About 40,000 children traveled the Oregon Trail. Except during the Gold Rush years when most travelers were single men, about one in five migrants were children.

- Making butter was one of the few easy tasks for pioneers on the trail. They put cream in a covered pail and hung it on the wagon. After a day on the trail, the constant jostling of the wagon turned the cream to butter.

- Many people who called themselves doctors traveled with the wagon trains along the Oregon and Santa Fe Trails. Many were self-taught or outright quacks and were more dangerous than the conditions they treated.

- Independence, Missouri, was founded in 1827. Five years later, it had become the center for supplies for wagon trains heading west and the beginning of both the Santa Fe and Oregon Trails for thousands of immigrants.

1. Use reference sources to find two other interesting bits of trail trivia.

   ____

   ____

   ____

   ____

   ____

2. As a class, combine your bits of trivia, form teams, and have a trail trivia tournament.

Name: ______________________________ Date: ______________________

Trail Math

Oregon Trail

The provisional government of Oregon allowed Samuel Barlow to open a toll road that provided an overland route around Mt. Hood to the Willamette Valley. With a crew of 40 men, he hacked out a narrow road about 150 miles long from The Dalles to Oregon City through forests and marshy meadows.

Barlow opened his road in 1846 and charged travelers $5 per wagon and 10 cents a head for livestock. Many people thought the road should be free, even though it was a safer route and less expensive than hiring men to take them down the dangerous Columbia River on rafts.

1. The first year, 145 wagons and 1,600 head of livestock used the road. How much did Barlow make that year? ______________________
2. The Mt. Hood Toll Road remained in use as a toll road until 1915. How many years was it used as a toll road? ______________________

Santa Fe Trail

Use the Santa Fe Trail mileage chart compiled by Alexander Dyer and published in *Stryker's American Register and Magazine* in 1850. This route began at Fort Leavenworth and shows the distance from Fort Leavenworth to Upper Ferry as 35 miles.

3. By the time travelers reached Council Grove, how far had they traveled from Fort Leavenworth? __________
4. How far was it from Lost Spring to the Pawnee Fork? __________
5. How far was it from Coon Creek to Middle Spring? __________
6. How far was it from Walnut Creek to Fort Mann? __________
7. How far was it from Bluff Creek to Cottonwood? __________
8. How far was it from Big Cow Creek to the Arkansas Crossing? __________
9. Which is closer to Main Turkey Creek: Big Cow Creek or Lost Spring? __________

Place	Distance in Miles
Upper Ferry	35
Willow Springs	17
110 Mile Creek	24
Beaver Creek	12
Dragoon Creek	8
Bluff Creek	13
Council Grove	12
Diamond Spring	15
Lost Spring	14
Cottonwood	15
Main Turkey Creek	18
Little Arkansas	26
Big Cow Creek	21
Walnut Creek	25
Pawnee Fork	25
Coon Creek	12
Fort Mann	55
Arkansas Crossing	26
Sand Creek	50
Lower Spring	8
Middle Spring	34
Santa Fe	no miles given

Name: ______________________ Date: ______________

Wagon Train Fact or Opinion?

A **fact** is a statement that can be verified as true.

Fact: Some wagons were pulled by oxen.

An **opinion** is a statement that cannot be verified as true.

Opinion: Oxen are better-tempered than mules.

Write *F* for fact or *O* for opinion on the line by each statement.

_____ 1. Millions of bison once roamed the plains.

_____ 2. Mountains, rivers, and deserts were difficult for wagons to cross.

_____ 3. Mountains are beautiful when covered with snow.

_____ 4. Children should not have been taken along on the Oregon or Santa Fe Trail because it was too dangerous.

_____ 5. Everyone who made the journey from Missouri to Oregon was very brave.

_____ 6. People hunted for bison, rabbit, squirrel, deer, and other animals along the trail.

_____ 7. Venison tastes better than squirrel or rabbit meat.

_____ 8. Sunrises are more beautiful than sunsets.

_____ 9. A herd of bison is an awesome sight.

_____ 10. Dried bison chips were used as fuel for fires.

11. Write two facts about the Oregon Trail. ______________________________

____

____

____

12. Write two opinions about the Santa Fe Trail. ______________________________

____

____

____

Name: ______________________________ Date: ______________________

Trail Sense

As people traveled west along the trails, they needed to acquire "trail sense." They had to learn how to do things they had never done before or how to do things in different ways, based on trail conditions.

People learned to hunt, cook, find water, and gather firewood as they traveled. They learned to build campfires, fix broken wagons, and take care of sick animals. They learned to predict the weather, locate edible plants, and find directions using the sun or stars.

1. List other skills people needed to survive along the trails.

____

____

____

Pioneers could determine the temperature in degrees Fahrenheit by listening to crickets. To do this, they counted the number of chirps in one minute, subtracted 40 from that number, divided by 4, then added 50.

Example: 60 chirps in one minute
Subtract 40 = 20
Divide by 4 = 5
Add 50 = 55°

2. Calculate the temperature in degrees Fahrenheit using this method.

   A. 64 chirps per minute

   Temperature ______________

   B. 80 chirps per minute

   Temperature ______________

3. Fill in the chart.

Temperature	50	52	54	56	58	60	62	64	66	68
Chirps/minute										

4. Why wouldn't this method work during the winter and when it was very cold?

____

____

If you have the opportunity, use a stopwatch and try this method for yourself. Compare your answer to the actual temperature.

Name: ______________________________ Date: ______________________

Cause and Effect

A **cause** is an event that produces a result. An **effect** is the result produced.

For each effect, write a possible cause.

	Possible Cause	Effect
1.	______________________	The wagon train was delayed several days because the river was swollen and impassable.
2.	______________________	Josh was extremely ill and had a high fever for a week.
3.	______________________	The pioneers had to throw away many treasured items in order to continue.
4.	______________________	The Johnsons decided to turn back.
5.	______________________	A wheel on the Morgans' wagon broke.
6.	______________________	The members of the wagon train ate well that night.
7.	______________________	Beth and Thomas had to walk barefoot the rest of the way.
8.	______________________	The snow piled up in drifts over eight feet high.

Name: ______________________________ Date: ____________________

True or False?

Circle *T* for True or *F* for False.

1. T F The Santa Fe Trail was shorter than the Oregon Trail.
2. T F Everyone who traveled west went with a wagon train.
3. T F Only Conestoga wagons were allowed on the Santa Fe Trail.
4. T F Deserts and canyons were two hazards settlers faced on the Oregon and Santa Fe Trails.
5. T F The Oregon and Santa Fe Trails mostly followed Native American trade routes and hunting trails.
6. T F Few children made the difficult journey across the Oregon and Santa Fe Trails.
7. T F Nine Men's Morris was a favorite stopping place along the Santa Fe Trail.
8. T F The settlers saw many elephants along the Oregon Trail.
9. T F Millions of bison once roamed the prairies of North America.
10. T F Diseases like cholera, influenza, scurvy, and malaria were common in the 1800s.
11. T F Settlers had to take all food and water for the entire journey, because there was no food or water along the way.
12. T F Some travelers preferred oxen rather than horses because oxen are stronger.
13. T F The Cimarron Cutoff was a shortcut on the Oregon Trail.
14. T F Most wagon trains began in Independence or St. Joseph, Missouri, or Council Bluffs, Iowa.
15. T F Conestoga wagons had six wheels rather than the usual four.

Name: ______________________________ Date: ____________________

Homonyms on the Trail

Homonyms are words that sound alike but are spelled differently and have different meanings.

Example: plains and planes

Write a homonym below each word listed. Then write a short definition for each word.

1. rains ____

   ____________ ________________________________

2. bear ____

   ____________ ________________________________

3. mail ____

   ____________ ________________________________

4. ware ____

   ____________ ________________________________

5. hare ____

   ____________ ________________________________

6. main ____

   ____________ ________________________________

7. clothes ____

   ____________ ________________________________

8. weather ____

   ____________ ________________________________

9. site ____

   ____________ ________________________________

10. peace ____

    ____________ ________________________________

Name: ______________________________ Date: ____________________

Similes and Metaphors

A **simile** is a figure of speech that uses *like* or *as* to compare two things that are not alike.

Example: The desert was **as dry as a bone**.

A **metaphor** is a figure of speech that uses a noun or noun phrase to make a direct comparison between two unlike things. The words *like* or *as* are not used in a metaphor.

Example: The woman was a **bundle of nerves** when she joined the wagon train.

Write *M* for metaphor or *S* for simile on the line before each sentence.

________ 1. The trip was a nightmare.

________ 2. The covered wagons were like ships as they crossed the plains.

________ 3. The desert was an oven.

________ 4. The desert was as hot as an oven.

________ 5. After the rain, the desert was a riot of color.

Finish the similes.

6. The wagon ride was as rough as ______________________________.
7. The flies were as thick as ______________________________.
8. Riding a mule was like ______________________________.
9. The sun was as hot as ______________________________.

Finish the metaphors.

10. The place they settled was ______________________________.
11. The weather in summer was ______________________________.
12. Crossing the desert was ______________________________.
13. The members of the wagon train were ______________________________.

Write two similes.

14. ____
15. ____

Write two metaphors.

16. ____
17. ____

Name: ______________________ Date: ______________

Who Took the Vowels?

Pioneers had to take most of their food for the journey, but those who knew what to look for and how to hunt could find some food along the trail.

Breadroot grows on prairies. Its tubers are edible. It can be cooked and eaten like potatoes.

Chicory is another prairie plant. Its leaves can be eaten like lettuce. The roots can be dug up, boiled, and eaten.

Someone took all the vowels from these items pioneers might have found along the trail. Fill in the blanks with "a," "e," "i," "o," or "u" to complete the words.

1. w ___ l d ___ n ___ ___ n s
2. b l ___ c k b ___ r r ___ ___ s
3. w ___ l d t ___ r k ___ y
4. p r ___ ___ r ___ ___ c h ___ c k ___ n
5. s q ___ ___ r r ___ l
6. h ___ r b s
7. ___ c ___ r n s
8. m ___ ___ s ___
9. r ___ d r ___ s p b ___ r r ___ ___ s
10. m ___ s h r ___ ___ m s
11. d ___ ___ r
12. f ___ s h
13. b ___ ___ r
14. b ___ s ___ n
15. n ___ t s
16. s n ___ k ___
17. g r ___ p ___ s
18. r ___ b b ___ t
19. ___ g g s
20. h ___ n ___ y

Name: ______________________ Date: ______________

In the News

A newspaper headline is a summary of the most important point in an article. Headlines must be brief, to-the-point, and grab the reader's attention.

Write headlines in eight words or less for each event.

1. Samuel Barlow opened the Mt. Hood Toll Road and began charging $5 per wagon and 10 cents per head for livestock. Many settlers were upset about the cost.

   ____

2. A new supply store opened in Independence, Missouri, where settlers could buy all the supplies needed for the trip to Oregon at a cost lower than anywhere else.

   ____

3. A wagon train that started out with 100 wagons and 524 people arrived in Santa Fe with only 24 wagons and 311 people. Those who completed the trip were extremely ill.

   ____

4. An epidemic of measles killed more than half of the Cayuse tribe, including most of the children. As a result, the Cayuse raided the Whitman Mission, killed 14 people, and burned the mission.

   ____

5. The Treaty of Guadalupe-Hidalgo marked the end of the Mexican War and provided for a payment of $15 million dollars by the United States to Mexico in exchange for control of California, Nevada, and Utah, plus parts of Colorado, Arizona, New Mexico, and Wyoming.

   ____

6. The "Great Migration" began when 1,000 settlers left Independence, Missouri, to begin the 2,000-mile trip to the Willamette Valley in 1843.

   ____

7. Free land was available in Oregon. Each married couple could claim up to 640 acres at no cost if they lived on it and cultivated it for four years.

   ____

Name: ______________________ Date: ______________________

Compound Capers

bonnet	box	cakes	camp	cat	deer
fall	fire	fish	light	mill	moon
news	pan	paper	pox	quick	rattle
sand	saw	set	skin	small	snake
sun	tool	water	wood		

Combine words from the box to make at least 15 compound words.

______________ ______________ ______________

______________ ______________ ______________

______________ ______________ ______________

______________ ______________ ______________

______________ ______________ ______________

Matching Activity

Match the words in the box with their definitions.

adobe	bison chips	Cimarron Cutoff	Conestoga wagons
Crack-the-Whip	diphtheria	Independence	prairie schooners
provisions	wagon jack	Willamette Valley	willow bark

1. ______________ nickname for white, canvas-topped wagons
2. ______________ a shortcut along the Santa Fe Trail
3. ______________ a game played by children
4. ______________ sun-dried bricks
5. ______________ destination of many settlers who went to Oregon
6. ______________ supplies
7. ______________ used for fuel
8. ______________ used to change a wheel on a covered wagon
9. ______________ type of transportation
10. ______________ a disease that could be fatal
11. ______________ used as a medicine
12. ______________ starting point for many wagon trains

Name: ______________________________ Date: ______________________

The Emigrants' Guide

Many guides to the Oregon and Santa Fe Trails were published. Some contained good advice about what to take and which routes to follow. However, some guides were written by people who had never experienced life on the trail. These guides could even be dangerous because they minimized the dangers, gave poor directions, and failed to include much that settlers needed to know to survive.

Write advice for a settler's guidebook for each topic.

1. Questions to ask yourself before you decide to join a wagon train:
____
____
2. What to expect on the trail: ______________________________
____
____
3. Items you MUST take: ______________________________
____
____
4. Items you should NOT take: ______________________________
____
____
5. Finding food along the trail: ______________________________
____
____
6. Advice for traveling uphill in a wagon: ______________________________
____
____
7. Advice for traveling downhill in a wagon: ______________________________
____
____
8. How to cross streams and rivers: ______________________________
____
____

Name: ______________________ Date: ______________________

Order, Please

Number the events in order from 1 (first) to 10 (last). Use the time line on pages 2 and 3 for reference.

_____ A. 1,000 settlers left Independence, Missouri, for the Willamette Valley in Oregon.

_____ B. California became a state.

_____ C. Abraham Lincoln was assassinated.

_____ D. Zebulon Pike explored most of the Santa Fe Trail.

_____ E. Gold was discovered at Sutter's Mill.

_____ F. Missouri became a state.

_____ G. Oregon became a state.

_____ H. The Transcontinental Railroad was completed.

_____ I. The Oregon Territory became part of the United States.

_____ J. Wisconsin became a state.

K. List two historical events that occurred **before** the events above.

____

____

____

L. List two historical events that occurred **after** the events above.

____

____

____

Challenge Question: How could people on a wagon train cook in a rainstorm?

____

____

____

Name: ______________________________ Date: ____________________

Scavenger Hunt

To complete this scavenger hunt, use the Internet and other reference materials to find the answers.

1. The first military fort built along the Oregon Trail to protect travelers was not walled. It was simply a collection of buildings, mostly made of sod. What was the name of the fort?

   ____

2. A treaty with several Native American tribes, including the Sioux, Cheyenne, Arapaho, and Crows, was signed at this fort in 1851. The Native Americans agreed to end hostilities among themselves and accept specific reservations in exchange for government protection from attacks by Whites and annual payments of money, food, goods, livestock, and tools. At what fort was this treaty signed?

   ____

3. Born in Kentucky in 1809, he ran away at the age of 17 to accompany hunters to Santa Fe. He made many trips to the West, hunting and trapping. He served as a guide to John Frémont on his mapping expeditions and was appointed as an Indian agent in 1854. Who was this mountain man?

   ____

4. This Missouri trader was the first to follow the route that later became the Santa Fe Trail. His mule train went through the area in 1821. He later took trade goods across the Santa Fe Trail using wagons. He is sometimes called the "Father of the Santa Fe Trail." What was his name?

   ____

5. Independence Rock was one of the most famous landmarks along the Oregon Trail. Here travelers rested, watered their livestock, and often carved their names and the date in the large rock that stood by itself. Because so many travelers carved their names in the rock, it acquired a nickname. What was the nickname given to Independence Rock?

   ____

6. Independence Rock is located on the north bank of a river in central Wyoming. Name the river.

   ____

7. Besides Independence Rock, there were two other outstanding natural monuments along the Oregon Trail: Chimney Rock and Red Buttes. In which state is Chimney Rock located?

   ____

8. In which state is Red Buttes located? ______________________________
9. Crossing the Jornada was a difficult part of the Santa Fe Trail because it is the northern part of a large desert. Name the desert.

   ____

Name: ____________________ Date: ____________

Then and Now

Traveling to Oregon, California, or Santa Fe today is much easier and quicker than it was in the 1840s. It's easy to forget the hardships the pioneers suffered as we drive down a smooth highway or fly across the country.

A car can travel the same distance in 15 or 20 minutes that it took a whole day for a wagon to travel. Hills and mountains present little difficulty for most modern vehicles. Bridges span even the shallowest rivers. Our vehicles are heated and air-conditioned. We can visit rest stops, stores, and restaurants along the way.

Along the old Oregon and Santa Fe Trails, you can still see some of the same landmarks the pioneers saw. In some places, you can see wheel ruts, depressions in the ground caused by the weight of wagons that once carried settlers and their goods west in search of a new life.

1. What is the distance from your home to Santa Fe? ____________________

2. Determine how long it would take to drive that far using 50 miles an hour as an average speed.

   ____

3. Use an Internet site or call a travel agent. Find out the cost of airfare from the nearest airport to any city in Oregon.

   ____

4. How long would the flight take? ____________________

5. What items that we take for granted today would not have been available to people traveling with a wagon train along the Oregon or Santa Fe Trail?

   ____________ ____________ ____________

   ____________ ____________ ____________

   ____________ ____________ ____________

   ____________ ____________ ____________

   ____________ ____________ ____________

Name: ______________________________ Date: ______________

Notable Names of the Western Trails

Learn more about a person who was involved with the westward movement and/or the western trails. Use the Internet and other reference sources to write a three- to five-page report about one of these people. Add illustrations and maps if possible. As an alternative activity, create a poster displaying pictures, drawings, maps, and information about one of the people on the list.

John Ashley
William Becknell
John Bidwell
Kit Carson
Buffalo Bill Cody
Mary Dodson Donoho
Thomas Fitzpatrick
Wild Bill Hickok
Jean Baptiste Lalande
Susan Shelby Magoffin
Zebulon Pike
Jedediah Smith
Marcus Whitman
"Uncle Dick" Wootton

Moses Austin
Charles Bent
Jim Bridger
George Catlin
Samuel Colt
Marie Dorion
John Frémont
Julia Archibald Holmes
Meriwether Lewis
Joe Meek
Marion Sloan Russell
General Zachary Taylor
Narcissa Whitman

Edward Beale
William Bent
Tabitha Moffat Brown
William Clark
John Colter
Abigail Scott Duniway
Josiah Gregg
Henrietta Chamberlain King
Major Stephen Long
Bethenia Owens-Adair
George Sibley
Pierre Louis Vasquez
Sarah Winnemucca

Sites Along the Trails

Learn more about a place along the Oregon or Santa Fe Trail. Use the Internet and other reference sources to write a report about one of these places. Include information about when it was founded, who founded it, and/or why it was of importance on one of the trails. Include illustrations and a map.

Ayres Natural Bridge
Caches
Clifton House
Fort Aubrey
Fort Dodge
Fort Larned
Fort Union
Fort Zarah
Independence Rock
Las Vegas (NM)
Platte River
St. Joseph
South Pass
Trinidad

Bent's New Fort
Chimney Rock
Council Spring
Fort Boise
Fort Kearny
Fort Lyon No. 2
Fort Vancouver
Glenn's Ferry
Jornada Desert
Ogallala
Raton Pass
Snake River
The Dalles

Bent's Old Fort
Cimarron
Diamond Spring
Fort Bridger
Fort Laramie
Fort Osage
Fort Walla Walla
Glorieta Pass
La Junta
Pawnee Rock
Red Buttes
Soda Springs
Three Crossings

Answer Keys

Manifest Destiny (page 5)

1. Manifest: apparent to the senses or to the mind; obvious; clear
   Destiny: the seemingly inevitable or necessary succession of events

From Missouri to Santa Fe (page 7)

1. Spain   2. Mexico
3. In 1848, the Treaty of Guadalupe-Hidalgo ended the Mexican War, and the United States gave Mexico $15 million for a large portion of what became the southwestern United States.
4. A mule train was a large number of mules traveling together carrying goods. Sometimes the mules were harnessed together in long "trains."
5. It was easier/quicker/cheaper to travel by train.

Along the Santa Fe Trail (page 8)

1. Teacher check map. 2. MO, KS, CO, NM
3. Teacher check map. 4. shorter 5. OK
6. Arkansas and Cimarron Rivers
7. CO 8. CO 9. NM 10. NM 11. KS
12. KS 13. MO 14. CO 15. KS

Native Americans in the East (page 10)

2. The governor thought white people had a right to all the land. Treaties were a way to trick Native Americans to give up the land without a fight.
3. Fight in court, go to war, hide in the hills, or give up and move.

The Trail of Tears (page 11)

1. The Native Americans were forced to leave thier land, homes, and most of their possessions. Thousands died on the way to the new Indian Territory.

Oregon Fever (page 12)

1. F 2. T 3. F 4. F 5. F 6. F 7. F

From Missouri to Oregon (page 13)

1. To blaze a trail means to be the first one to find a way through an unexplored area.
2. Wyoming 3. Wind River Range
4. Snake River 5. Blue Mountains

Along the Oregon Trail (page 14)

1. Teacher check map.
2. KS, NE, WY, ID, WA
3. WY 4. OR 5. NE 6. NE
7. WY 8. ID 9. NE 10. WY
11. MO 12. ID 13. ID 14. OR 15. ID

Getting From Here to There (page 16)

Santa Fe Trail:

A. 2 B. 5 C. 7 D. 3 E. 1
F. 4 G. 9 H. 8 I. 6

Oregon Trail:

J. 4 K. 6 L. 9 M. 2 N. 5
O. 1 P. 10 Q. 8 R. 7 S. 3

In Search of Religious Freedom (page 17)

1. The state or practice of having two or more spouses at the same time
2. NY, OH, MO, IL
3. Outrage against polygamy; resented that church members tended to buy only from Latter-day Saints-owned businesses; Latter-day Saints all voted for the same person; communal ownership of property that they could redistribute to those in need

The Latter-day Saints Move West (page 18)

1. They would need enough food and wagons. They couldn't make the trip in one year, so they had to camp for the winter where many died. They had to find their way to Salt Lake. He had to coordinate thousands of people moving from Illinois to Salt Lake over several years. He had to arrange for temporary quarters in Missouri for converts from other countries.
2. Clear land, lay out streets, find water sources, build houses, grow crops, form a government, set up businesses, create a sewer system, etc.

The Forty-Niners (page 20)

1. Methods of travel were slow, and they came from hundreds to thousands of miles away.
2. Jason; the Golden Fleece
3. They were heading out on a wild adventure looking for gold.

Along the California Trail Map (page 22)

1. California Trail, Old Spanish Trail
2. Approx. 1,600 miles
3. Wagon train: 4–5 months; Stagecoach: 1 month; Clipper Ship: 100 days

Decisions, Decisions (page 23)

2. A. Horses: Advantages: fastest
   Disadvantages: not as strong as oxen, required more food, more expensive
   B. Oxen: Advantages: strongest, required the least food, least expensive
   Disadvantages: slowest, more sensitive to heat and dust
   C. Mules: Advantages: required less food than horses, faster than oxen
   Disadvantages: more expensive than oxen, not as strong as oxen, could be stubborn to handle since they would refuse to cross dangerous terrain

Conestoga Wagons (page 24)

1. They were named after the Conestoga River or Township in Lancaster, PA, where German settlers made the wagons.

The Cost of Supplies (page 26)

1. $180 2. 4 oxen 3. $21
4. $6.35 5. 10 pounds of beans
6. 50 cents
7. Added cost of shipping the materials or finished nails

What Is It? (page 33)

1. Ox yoke: used to control a pair of oxen
2. Horseshoe: used to protect horses' feet
3. Razor strop: used to sharpen razors for shaving
4. Whetstone: used to sharpen knives
5. Wagon jack: used to help remove, repair, and replace wagon wheels
6. Wheel rim: iron band placed around a wooden wheel for strength
7. Spinning wheel: used to spin thread or yarn
8. Wooden barrel: used to store water, flour, and other items

Where the Bison Once Roamed (page 36)

1. Answers could include: food, hides for covering tipis or other shelters, clothing made from hides, soap made from the fat, tools made from the bones, bladder used as a bag, hair used to make rope, etc.

The End of the Trail (page 40)

2. To encourage people to settle in the west.
3. *Adobe* is a Spanish word meaning "sun-dried clay."
4. Settlers mixed clay and water and then added sand, plant roots, and/or straw for strength. They poured the mixture into wooden molds and left the bricks to harden in the sun. They stacked the bricks to make thick walls, and then they made a plaster of clay and water to smooth over the bricks. Sometimes animals' blood was mixed with the clay to make it harder and less likely to turn to mud when it rained.

Building Wooden Homes (page 41)

2. machete-type knife, clippers, rakes, axes, etc.
3. axes, saws, drawing knives, animals to move the logs, etc.
4. A. 7 or 8 B. 4 C. 2 D. 5 E. 3 F. 6 G. 7 or 8 H. 1

From Pittsburgh to the Willamette Valley (page 42)

A. 3 B. 6 C. 9 D. 7 E. 11 F. 1 G. 14
H. 12 I. 8 J. 10 K. 13 L. 5 M. 2 N. 4

Pioneer Medicine (page 43)

1. Camphor was used to treat colds.
2. It is very addictive. 3. malaria 4. aspirin

Trail Math (page 45)

1. $885 2. 69 years 3. 121 miles
4. 130 miles 5. 173 miles 6. 92 miles
7. 56 miles 8. 143 miles 9. Lost Spring

Wagon Train Fact or Opinion? (page 46)

1. F 2. F 3. O 4. O 5. O 6. F 7. O
8. O 9. O 10. F

Trail Sense (page 47)

1. Answers may include fishing, cleaning game, tanning hides, making jerky, sewing canvas, fording rivers, etc.
2. A. 56° B. 60°
3. 40, 48, 56, 64, 72, 80, 88, 96, 104, 112
4. Crickets are not active when it is cold.

True or False? (page 49)

1. T 2. F 3. F 4. T 5. T 6. F 7. F
8. F 9. T 10. T 11. F 12. T 13. F 14. T
15. F

Homonyms on the Trail (page 50)

1. reigns/reins 2. bare 3. male
4. wear/where 5. hair 6. mane/Maine
7. close 8. whether/wether
9. cite/sight 10. piece

Similes and Metaphors (page 51)

1. M 2. S 3. M 4. S 5. M

Who Took the Vowels? (page 52)

1. wild onions 2. blackberries 3. wild turkey
4. prairie chicken 5. squirrel 6. herbs
7. acorns 8. moose 9. red raspberries
10. mushrooms 11. deer 12. fish
13. bear 14. bison 15. nuts
16. snake 17. grapes 18. rabbit
19. eggs 20. honey

Compound Capers (page 54)

Accept all reasonable answers. Possible words are: campfire, catfish, deerskin, firewood, moonlight, newspaper, pancakes, quicksand, rattlesnake, sawmill, smallpox, snakeskin, sunbonnet, sunfish, sunlight, sunset, toolbox, waterfall

Matching Activity (page 54)

1. prairie schooners 2. Cimarron Cutoff
3. Crack-the-Whip 4. adobe
5. Willamette Valley 6. provisions
7. bison chips 8. wagon jack
9. Conestoga wagons 10. diphtheria
11. willow bark 12. Independence

Order, Please (page 56)

A. 3 B. 7 C. 9 D. 1 E. 5 F. 2 G. 8
H. 10 I. 4 J. 6

Scavenger Hunt (page 57)

1. Fort Kearny 2. Fort Laramie
3. Kit Carson 4. William Becknell
5. Register of the Desert 6. Sweetwater River
7. Nebraska 8. Wyoming
9. Chihuahua Desert

Suggested Reading

Songs of the Wild West by Alan Axelrod
Frontier Home by Raymond Bial
Westward Ho!: An Activity Guide to the Wild West by Laurie Carlson
California Gold Rush: Search for Treasure by Catherine E. Chambers
Settling the American West by James L. Collins
The Black Cowboys by Gina De Angelis
Daily Life in a Covered Wagon by Paul Erickson
The Story of Women Who Shaped the West by Mary Virginia Fox
Children of the Wild West by Russell Freedman
Homes of the West by Bobbie Kalman
The Gold Rush by Bobbie Kalman
Wagon Train by Bobbie Kalman
Pioneer Days: Discover the Past with Fun Projects, Games, Activities, and Recipes by David C. King
The Way West: Journal of a Pioneer Woman by Amelia Stewart Knight
If You Traveled West in a Covered Wagon by Ellen Levine
Meet the Wards on the Oregon Trail by John J. Loeper
Buffalo Gals: Women of the Old West by Brandon Marie Miller
How Would You Survive in the American West? by Jacqueline Morley
West by Covered Wagon: Retracing the Pioneer Trails by Dorothy Hinshaw Patent
Black Heroes of the Wild West by Ruth Pelz
Westward on the Oregon Trail by Marian T. Place
A Multicultural Portrait of the Move West by Petra Press
Brigham Young: Pioneer and Mormon Leader by William R. Sanford and Carl R. Green
A Frontier Fort on the Oregon Trail (Inside Story) by Scott Steedman
The Story of the Trail of Tears by R. Conrad Stein
The Pioneers Go West by George Rippey Stewart
Fantastic Facts About the Oregon Trail by Michael Trinklein

Fiction:

Across the Wide and Lonesome Prairie: The Oregon Trail Diary of Hattie Campbell, 1847 by Kristiana Gregory
Seeds of Hope: The Gold Rush Diary of Susanna Fairchild, California Territory, 1849 by Kristiana Gregory
For Ma and Pa On the Oregon Trail by Wilma Pitchford Hays
Tree in the Trail by Clancy Holling
Facing West: A Story of the Oregon Trail by Kathleen Kudlinski
All the Stars in the Sky: The Santa Fe Trail Diary of Florrie Mack Ryder, The Santa Fe Trail, 1848 by Megan McDonald
Rachel's Journal: The Story of a Pioneer Girl by Marissa Moss
Lucretia Ann on the Oregon Trail by Ruth Gipson Plowhead
The Girl Who Chased Away Sorrow: The Diary of Sarah Nita, a Navajo Girl, New Mexico, 1864 by Ann Turner
Bound for Oregon by Jean Van Leeuwen